michele de lucchi

Silvia Suardi

michele de lucchi
Dopotolomeo

SKIRA

Graphic Concept
Michele De Lucchi
Silvia Suardi

Layout
Stefano Tosi
Sara Salvi

Editing
Giorgio Bigatti

Translations from Italian
Language Consulting Congressi srl

Cover
Lamp Tolomeo, 1986
Sketch by Michele De Lucchi

First published in Italy in 2002
by Skira Editore S.p.A.
Palazzo Casati Stampa
via Torino 61
20123 Milano
Italy

Printed and bound in Italy. First edition

ISBN 88-8491-297-0

Distributed in North America and Latin
America by Rizzoli International Publications,
Inc. through St. Martin's Press, 175 Fifth
Avenue, New York, NY 10010.
Distributed elsewhere in the world by Thames
and Hudson Ltd., 181a High Holborn, London
WC1V 7QX, United Kingdom.

Contents

DOPOTOLOMEO

Dopotolomeo, far from being an astronomical dissertation, instead refers to the "aftermath" of a lamp, and more precisely to what has happened in the professional life of Michele De Lucchi from the birth of the famous Tolomeo until today.

Dopotolomeo is a diary that is as sincere and messy as the succession of events of life; it is a collage of images and thoughts, as chaotic as anything that comes to life in people's heads. The thread of this diary is drawn from the notebooks that De Lucchi has kept ever since his time at university: from the first one on squared paper for his accounts, to the larger ones with paper for water-colours, to the "small notebooks", packed with words, which now represent Michele De Lucchi's professional history.

His work, but also his life.

"They have been my lifeline, my 47 notebooks of sketches – a line that holds all my work together and keeps its evolution comprehensible amid the succession of changes – I am still using no. 48. I keep them on my bookshelves, together with the small notebooks, the diaries, the files where I try to organise the sketches in various orders, sometimes by project, at others by object typology, at others still by the name of the company or client."

These notebooks contain a universe rich in thoughts, anecdotes, photos, literary quotations, sketches, impressions. They tell of the everyday life of Michele De Lucchi mixed with his projects, his work linked with his life, his way of perceiving the world and his things, his most intimate and confidential soul.

Or perhaps it would be better to say his two souls, those that De Lucchi always makes coexist and that probably constitute the richness of his work: one linked to the research from the Memphis period to Produzione Privata and the other, the professional one of the architect who designed the branches of the Deutsche Bank and the ticket offices of the Deutsche Bundesbahn, the offices of the Italian Post Office and Enel plants.

As De Lucchi says, "this is a splendid opportunity to sort out the things in my house."

Dopotolomeo follows the spirit of his notebooks, a free and intimate spirit, as his diaries always are. It is a collection of images, drawings, photos, four-leafed clovers and quotations, illustrious phrases and simple impressions of a happy day in the sun. It is in the shadow of the most private thoughts and water-colours that the great projects come to life, and so there is an alternation of images, overlapping or adjacent, of transparent vases and power stations, of banks and blown glass lamps, of electricity pylons and mechanisms for the Tolomeo.

If we observe De Lucchi's work, we do not perceive a formal continuity, but rather a continuity of thought, "der rote Faden," the red thread, that connects up all his works. A same wavelength, a conceptual union that is translated into different formal approaches according to the changing times and moments. A "De Lucchi style" probably does not exist, because, as he himself says, "it is not only the form that makes things beautiful." It is not the formal aspect that is the most fascinating, but the capacity to grasp the "Zeitgeist," the spirit of the age, and to translate it, on each occasion, into different signs.

The flow of the images of Dopotolomeo is reminiscent of a karstic river, in which the messages sometimes appear very clear, immediate – the analogies to the anthropomorphous forms of many of his projects – and others are more subtended, hidden, underground. Yet the river keeps on flowing and a little further on it resurfaces, carrying along its history, a continuous flow, even if made of discontinuity, because "it is an essential part of making projects to produce and sustain reasons of discontinuity."

The great themes highlighted in Dopotolomeo represent the exposed part of his work: it is a transversal reading that enables us to look between the lines to see the submerged thoughts, the sense of change, the value of quality.

"Today the only certainty," says De Lucchi, "is that everything is changing and will change again when it has been changed: my objective is to participate in the change and to support the mutation. Change is the reason of life. Even what seemed to be great unchangeable certainties are no longer so: comfort, functionalism, ergonomics and – last but not least – beauty, are variable parameters. The certainty that we will not longer be as we were before makes attitudes change with things, and since I must design things, I must understand why this happens."

In the past it was art that represented a period, while now this role has been taken on by design. Today industrial products are the most recognisable signs of a period, those that best encapsulate the spirit of the age, that is, those emotions, those evocations, those tastes, those immaterial but strong signs that make an object belong to a period and charge it with all the meanings of the historical moment.

The figure of the designer-architect is therefore redefined: no longer the image of the isolated artist who designed in solitude, but rather the ideal bridge between industry and humanity, between company and consumer.

"The designer is much more fully inserted in the industry," says De Lucchi. "He belongs to the processes of business development, which is precisely why I think that design always represents an open debate and therefore that it is precisely the role of the designer to activate the debate… If in the past it was the artist who showed people the beauties of nature, now it is the designer who must show people the beauties of technology."

And this is what we find in Dopotolomeo, the figure of the architect for industry, of whom Peter Behrens was the precursor, the contemporary professional who moves with agility among the prototypes of Murano blown glass, as well as among the great electricity plants of Enel, who designs a Fata for his Produzione Privata and multifunctional faxes for Olivetti, who lives the project from the ideal poetry of the water-colour, "an intimate, deep, personal and sensual thing," to the realistic renderings generated on the computer – "because today we can no longer do without the computer."

Everything, always, in search of a changed sense of things, to find and reach expressions in which a new formula of richness is manifested, because "the sense of things lies neither in the production plants, nor on the shelves of supermarkets, nor in our homes or offices: it is much closer, much more available, much more within our grasp than we think. It is in our heads, in our imagination, in our desires and our expectations. This, then, is the role that I have given to myself and it is the definition of what I do that most satisfies me when I say that I try to give a sense to things; I look for it in people's heads and I grab it before anyone else does it before me."

TOLOMEO

Tolomeo is the lamp designed by Michele De Lucchi in 1986, which met with enormous and unexpected success, to the extent that De Lucchi is accustomed to saying, "if I had understood how I designed the Tolomeo, I would have designed some others."

"Designing lamps is my hobby in a way: I have designed plenty of them," continues De Lucchi, "and the most difficult of them all are certainly swing-arm table lamps. I have failed many times in this challenge, with lamps that worked for a while and then collapsed miserably, burning out the bulb, and with others that worked very well, but for some reason did not sell at all. With the Tolomeo I have redeemed myself."

The first idea came to me when watching a fisherman laboriously casting a rod to hoist his net. To make his operation easier, he had fixed the pole to the ground and hoisted it by throwing a rope that moved along a pulley fixed to the top of the pole. "It seemed intelligent to me," says De Lucchi, "that, with a small lever arm and a cable, a pole could be suspended to which to attach something; I have used this intuition to design not a simple lamp but the updated version of the famous, greatly used, big selling swing-arm lamp by Naska Loris, the so-called architects' lamp, because there would be no architect's table if not for Naska Loris. There was not, because today, fortunately, everyone - or almost - has the Tolomeo."

An important contribution to the success of the Tolomeo comes from the flexibility and adaptability of this lamp. Since its presentation on the market, many versions have been introduced: table, wall, floor, reading, spot, clamp-on, with halogen light bulb and low energy consumption fluorescent light bulb. Recently the micro version has been launched, with shorter arms and smaller head: a miniature Tolomeo.

Today the Tolomeo is the biggest selling contemporary design lamp in the world. We find it everywhere in our daily lives: from the office to the home, to museums, in a suitable setting in a modern context or an old-fashioned environment, in a banker's office or the most futuristic space capsule.

The symbol of the modern object, it is often used in photo shoots for consumer, fashion and furnishing products, and we discover it in the set designs of international cinema productions, from our own film productions to those of Asian cinema.

"Yet," says De Lucchi, "it is really a mundane table lamp, with a very simple form and an intelligent mechanism to make it stand. It is all made of aluminium, and perhaps for this reason it is so popular among architects."

This lamp has been decisive, not so much because of its symbolic character, as for the definition of De Lucchi's professional life, to the extent that it marked a turning point and defined a watershed between everything that had been done before and what was to be done afterwards.

The Tolomeo marks a crucial moment of transition: for De Lucchi the current of research and experimentation of Memphis flowed into a different formal path that was capable of expressing his character, his thought and his sensibility better. Products, environments and architectures were created that were less surprising but more personal, richer in contents, more studied and also more problematic, more loaded with technology and innovation.

The Tolomeo represents this passage, with its air of modernity perhaps linked to the material — aluminium — with the technology enclosed in a small unseen mechanism, and with its elegant shape: a sure and light sign that defines a mysterious and seductive object.

The Tolomeo contains a sea change within itself and is perhaps something more: it is the meeting point between two worlds, the office and the home, which, with farsighted vision, De Lucchi hypothesised, in a near future, ever closer to each other, increasingly interconnected.

Approximately two decades have gone by from the birth of the Tolomeo. This is the opportunity to stop and see what the situation is, it is the moment to understand what happened afterwards.

5 October 1996, Bonn, Conference on desing

IF YOU ASK ME WHAT JOB I ACTUALLY DO, I DON'T KNOW HOW TO ANSWER, BECAUSE IN FACT I REALLY DON'T KNOW AND DON'T
WANT TO KNOW, IN ORDER NOT TO BECOME SLAVE TO ONE TRADE SECTOR; I AM CONTENTED AND MAKE IT A POINT OF PRIDE TO KNOW
THAT I AM FREE, NAKED AND HAPPY IN MY RELATIONS WITH THE WORLD, WHICH THINKS IT CAN SURPRISE ME AT ANY MOMENT.

michele de lucchi

6 GENN 89

1. architecture

IT IS BEAUTIFUL TO SEE THE OUTSIDE OF THE HOUSE FROM INSIDE

15 October 1990, notebook no. 10

I have understood that for me architecture is construction, that is, putting stone on stone and element on element, and I have begun to draw and draw. It was in summer, I was in the country and I designed houses in the country in a climate of summer. The joy of designing spaces and architectures is always mixed with the fun of drawing, and perhaps for this reason my houses are always in nature and always constitute a bond between artificial and natural space. In design after design I have been able to focus on the elements of my architecture, which have flowed above all into the firm determination to avoid the volumes on which to compose graphics, which is what is learnt in schools and which all realise in the profession. My houses are always born from the earth and the elements on the ground act as supports for those above, which in turn support those higher above, and so on. This effect is always emphasised as far as possible. Openings and windows thus come about spontaneously, as residual spaces between architectural elements and there is no need for further processes of composition in the graphics of façades.

This system allows very rigorous and simple spaces to be constructed, but at the same time ones that are rich and highly structured. It enables you to have architectures in which the construction concept is always conscious and the compositional laws are always recognised.

and/of slabs

1

2

3

Gunma
Japan

16·III
1991

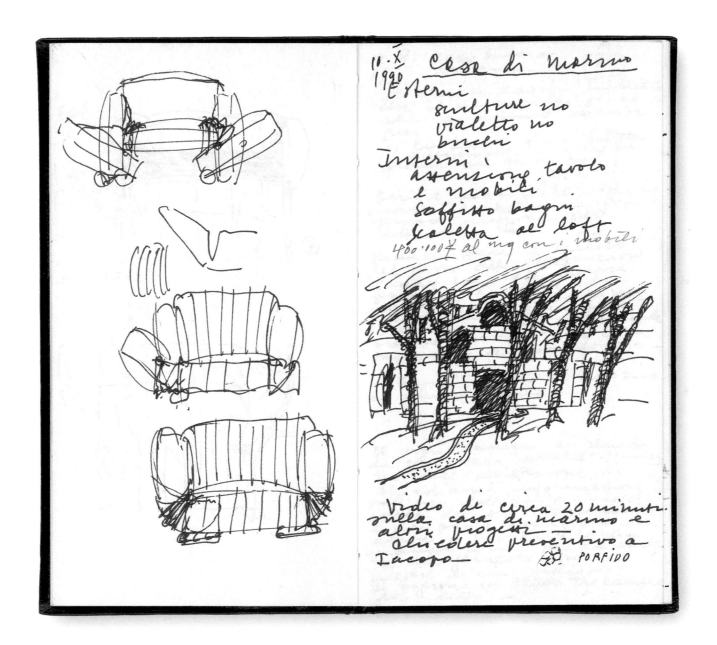

11·X
1990

Casa di marmo

Esterni
    sculture no
    vialetto no
    bucci

Interni
    ascensione, tavolo
    e mobili
    soffitto bagni
    scaletta al loft
    400·100£ al mq con i mobili

Video di circa 20 minuti.
sulla casa di marmo e
altri progetti —
    chiedere preventivo a
Iacopo —   PORFIDO

HISTORY IS NOT ONLY THE PAST, BUT THE AWARENESS OF WHERE WE

ARE, WHERE WE COME FROM, AND ABOVE ALL WHERE WE WANT TO GO

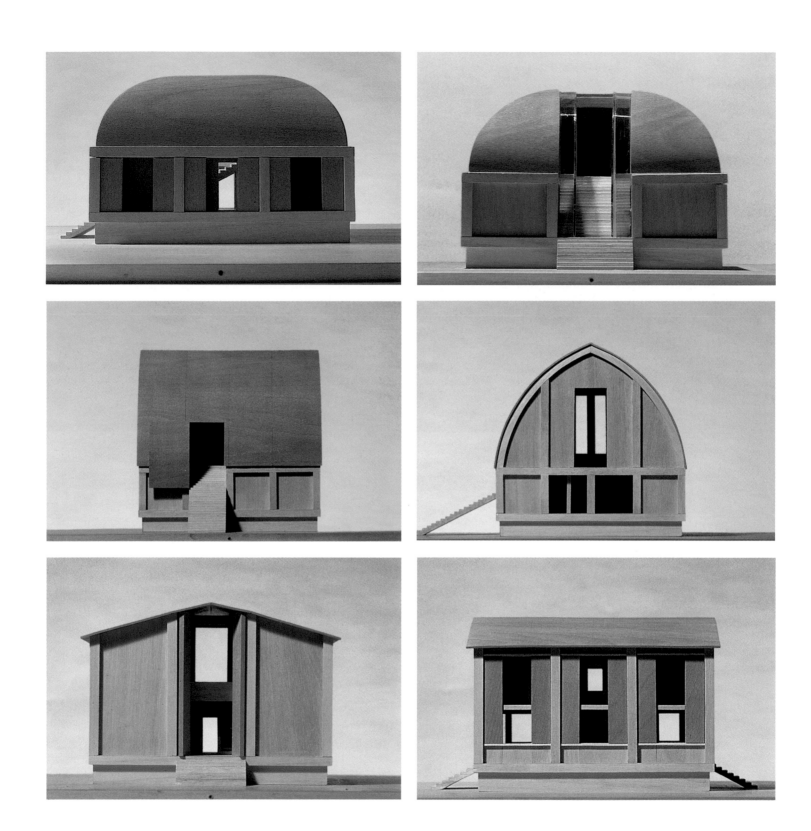

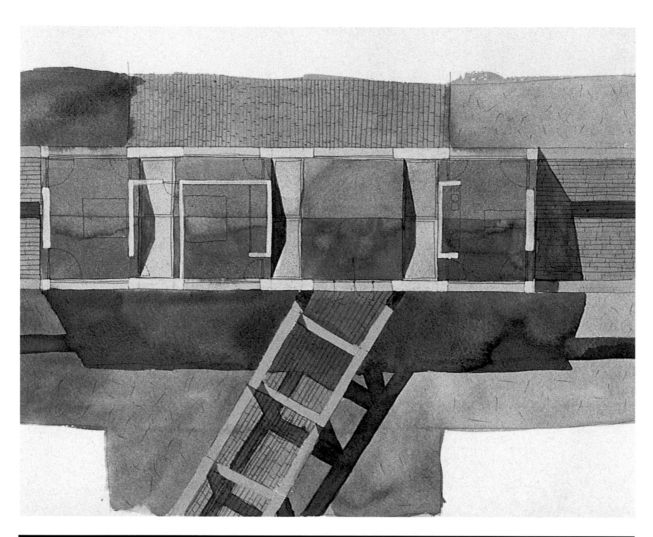

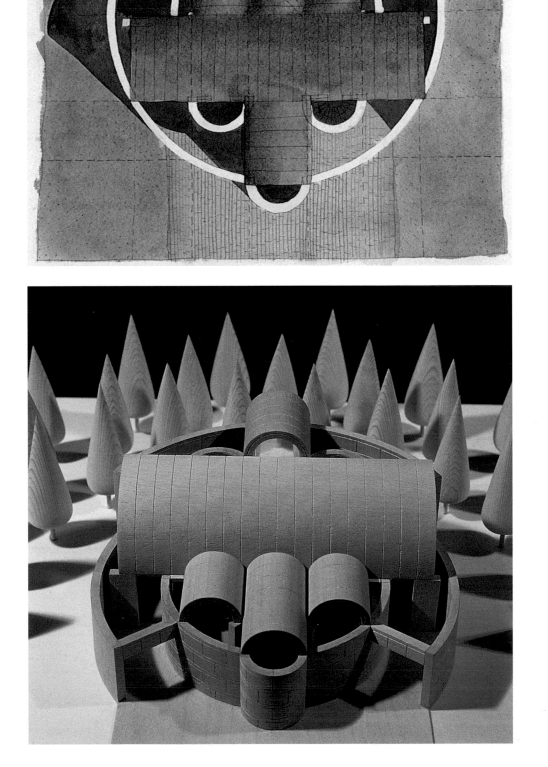

20 January 1997

I would like to say that the most beautiful and extraordinary material that exists, more pre-

cious and rare, supple, flexible and recyclable, is neither plastic, nor aluminium, nor some

alloy of metals and resins, nor an ultra technological compound that no one has invented

yet, but space, air, the air we breathe and in which we walk, the air that we buy and sell

and sculpt as though it were wax and so long as it is around, we do not worry about it, but

when it will be gone we will not know where to go to find it and it cannot be produced in a

factory. And then there is also another material, also expensive, which we already never

have now, and which we use very badly and unfortunately is not recyclable (but this is also a

fortune) and that is time.

TO EXPRESS A SERVICE IS IN ITSELF VERY SIMPLE, JUST AS IT IS SIMPLE TO SELL A TICKET, TO CHANGE MONEY IN THE BANK, TO SELL A FLIGHT OR TO HIRE OUT A CAR, TO OFFER THE STIPULATION OF AN INSURANCE CONTRACT OR AN INTEGRATED PENSION. THE DIFFICULTY IS TO GIVE PERSONALITY TO THIS SERVICE BY INTERVENING IN ALL THOSE ASPECTS NOT DIRECTLY CONNECTED TO THE BUSINESS BUT COMPLEMENTARY TO IT, ESPECIALLY IN RELATION TO THE ATMOSPHERE AND THE MANAGEMENT OF THE PERCEPTIONS THAT STRIKE THE CUSTOMER THROUGHOUT THE PERIOD WHEN THE STRUCTURE OF THE SERVICE IS USED. THE PROBLEM OF THE DESIGN OF SERVICES UNDERSTOOD IN THIS WAY IS DECIDEDLY A PROBLEM OF ARCHITECTURE, NOT SO MUCH OF CONSTRUCTION, AS OF THE CAPACITY TO INTERVENE IN ALL THE SENSORY ASPECTS OF THE SPECIFIC PLACE. IT MEANS KNOWING HOW TO WORK WELL, NOT ONLY WITH THE WALLS, NOT ONLY WITH THE MATERIALS, NOT ONLY WITH THE FURNISHINGS, BUT ESPECIALLY WITH THE SO-CALLED "SOFT" PARAMETERS, THAT IS, THE LIGHT, COLOUR, WARMTH, SMELL, AND GRADUALLY THE SENSE OF WELCOMING, EFFICIENCY, AGREEABILITY, COMFORT, ETC. AND NOT ONLY THIS; THE PROBLEM OF THE DESIGN

2. identity, charac

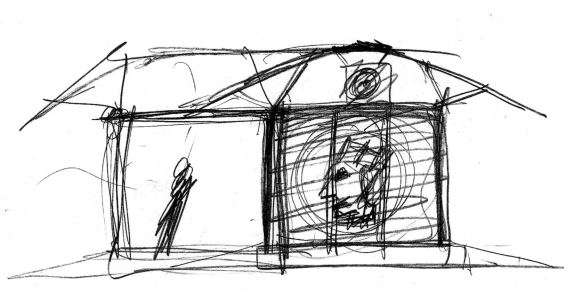

OF SERVICES IS A PROBLEM OF INDUSTRIALISATION, BECAUSE THE PLACES OF SERVICES ARE IN MOST CASES CONCERNS THAT ARE REPEATED ON SEVERAL OCCA-

SIONS, AND THE MORE THE CONCERNS ARE REPEATED, THE MORE NECESSARY AND URGENT BECOMES CO-ORDINATION AND THE REQUIREMENT TO MAKE SER-

VICES BELONGING TO THE SAME CATEGORY, INSTITUTION OR ORGANISATION ALWAYS RECOGNISABLE AND HOMOGENEOUS. HOWEVER, THE MOST IMPORTANT

ASPECT IN PROJECTS OF THIS KIND IS ONCE AGAIN RELATIVE TO COMMUNICATION AND THE CAPACITY TO INFORM ON WHAT EVERY SIGN, EVERY ARCHITECTURAL

CHOICE, EVERY FORMAL INVENTION MUST HAVE WITH RESPECT TO THE CENTRAL THEME. THE PLACES OF THE SERVICE ARE PLACES OF GREAT TENSION, WHERE

THE EVOLUTION AND SOPHISTICATION THAT THE CONTEMPORARY WORLD REQUIRES ARE EXPRESSED IN THE CONCENTRATION AND THE CONTEMPORARY EFFEC-

TIVENESS OF ALL THE MESSAGES THAT WE COULD CALL INDIRECT. YET INDIRECT DOES NOT MEAN SECONDARY; RATHER, AS OFTEN HAPPENS IN LANGUAGE, IT IS

THE DEEPEST AND LEAST EXTERNAL CONCEPTS THAT GIVE THE TRUE MEANING TO THINGS.

ter, personality

Poste**italiane**   199

Prodotti BancoPosta

Uscita

Roma 1

INDUSTRIAL DESIGN IS DIFFERENT FROM ARCHITECTURE, BUT IT IS LIKE ARCHITECTURE. THERE IS IN FACT THE

DESIGN BORN FROM THE "PRIMORDIAL SOUP" OF THE PROBLEM, OF FORM, OF TECHNOLOGY, AND THE ONE

BORN FROM THE "PRIMORDIAL SOUP" OF ARCHITECTURE. THE TWO APPROACHES ARE VERY DIFFERENT AND

RARELY MEET. PERSONALLY I BELONG TO THE GROUP OF DESIGNER-ARCHITECTS, BECAUSE ITALY IS A COUN-

TRY WITH LITTLE TECHNOLOGY AND THEREFORE TECHNOLOGICAL TEACHING DOES NOT EXIST. I AM VERY

HAPPY AND SATISFIED, HOWEVER, BECAUSE I THINK THAT THE ATTITUDE OF AN ARCHITECT-DESIGNER IS

RICHER AND I THINK THAT IN THE FUTURE THESE HUMANISTIC VALUES WILL BE APPRECIATED VERY MUCH.

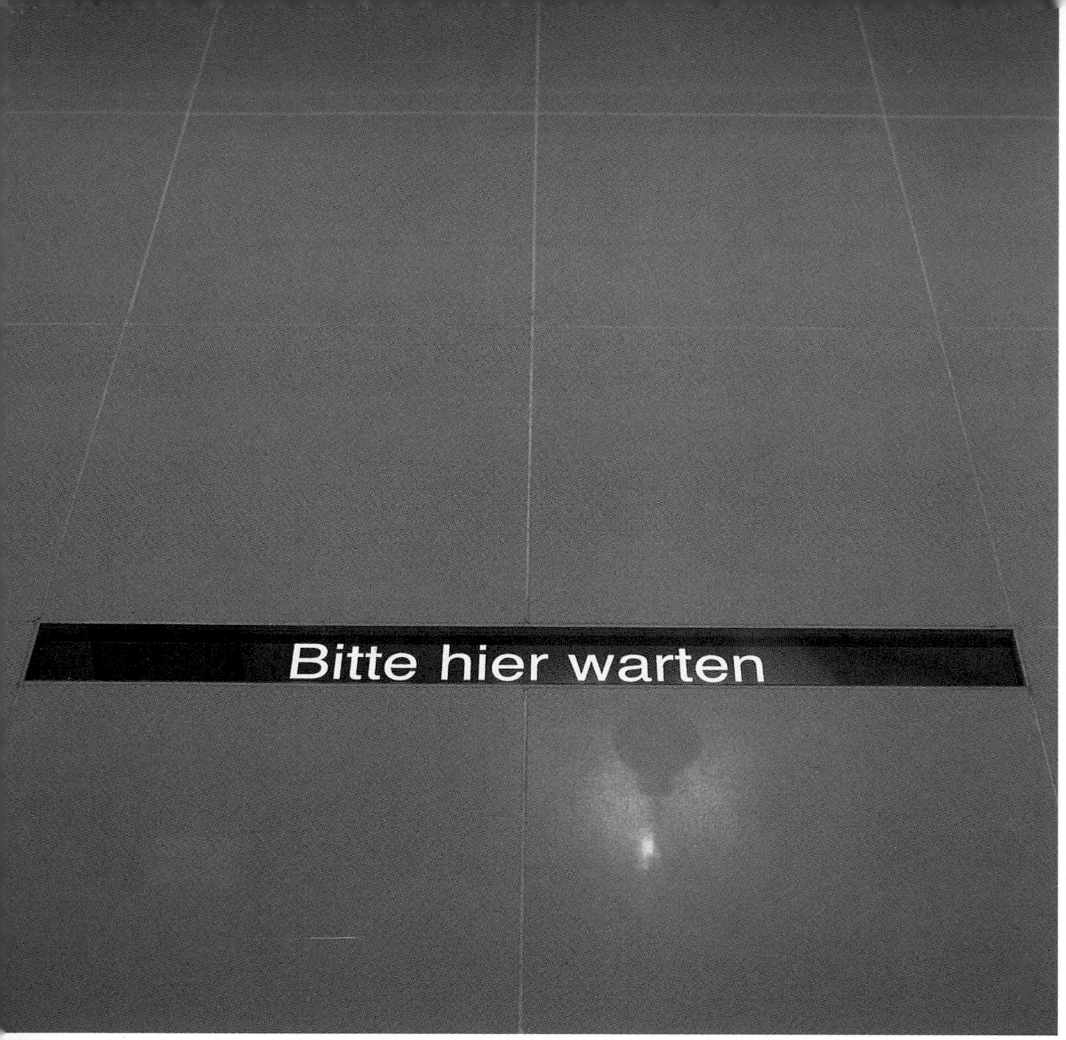
Bitte hier warten
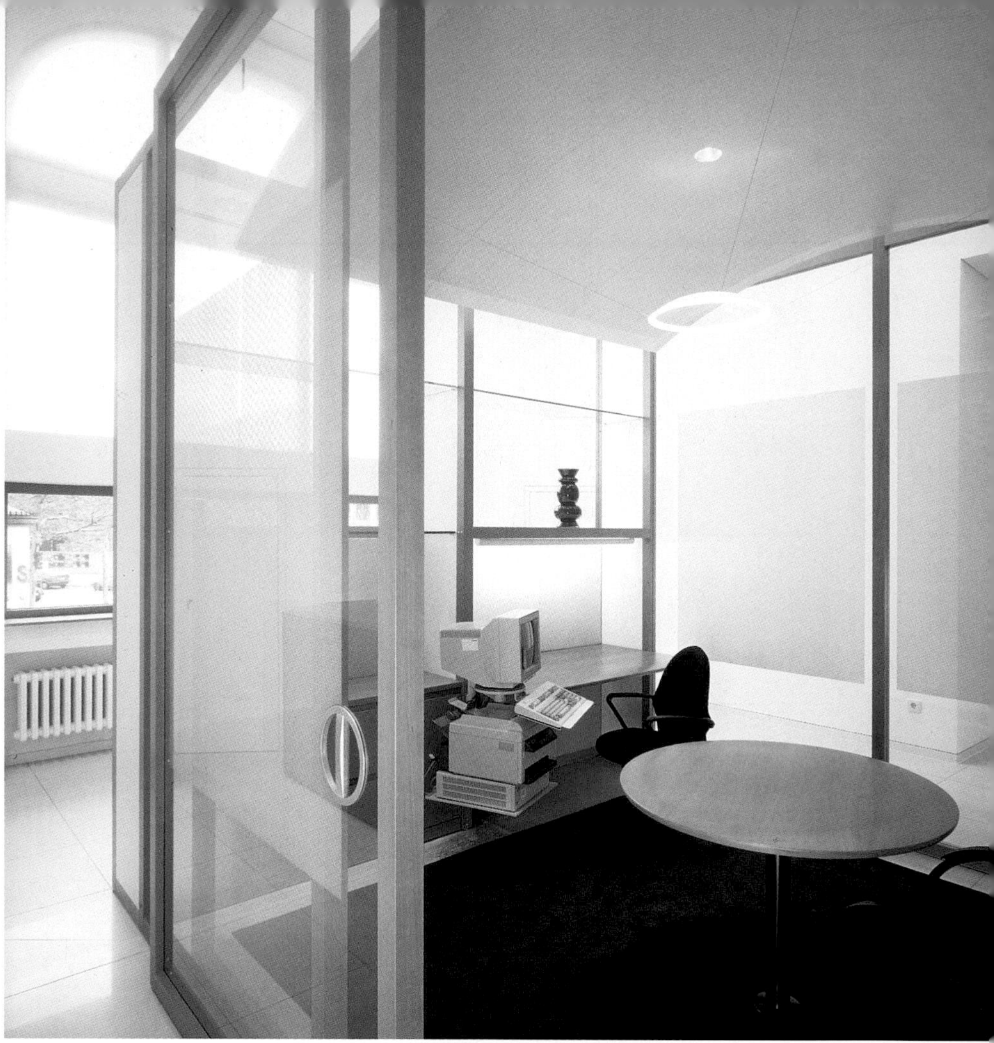
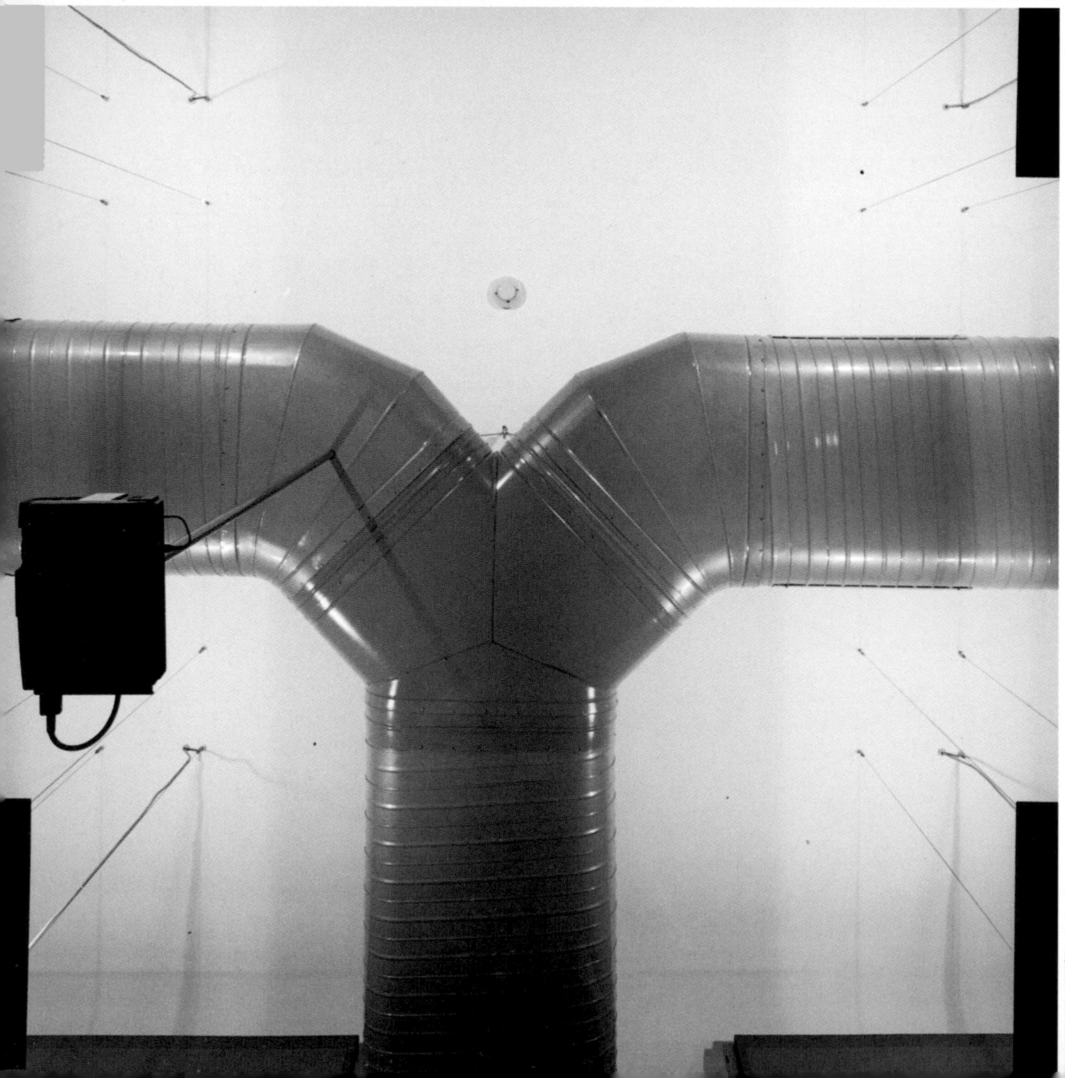
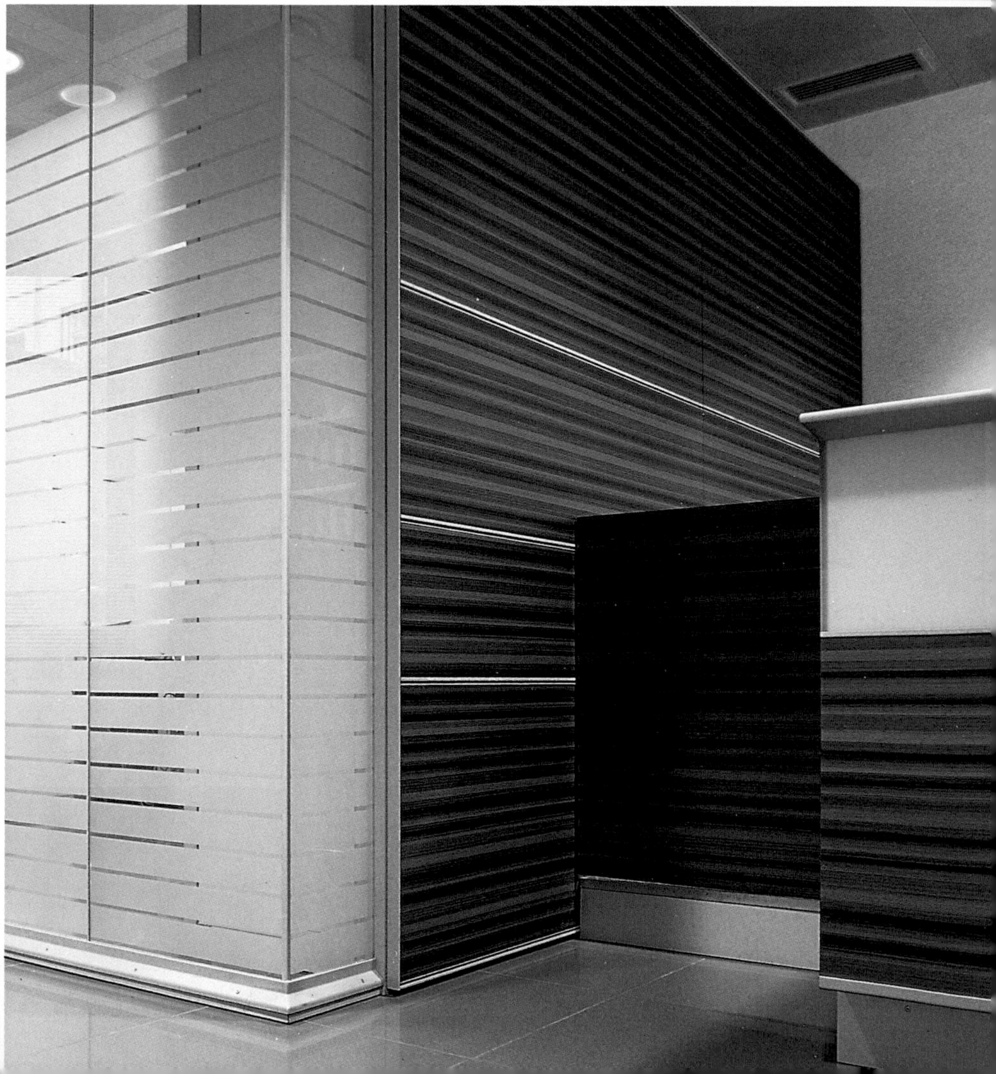

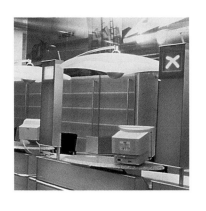

To be a good designer, you need to love industry

and be aware that there is no alternative to industry and consumerism.

It is not the designer's task to refound capitalist and consumer society, but simply

TO GIVE QUALITY
to consumerism

I feel a great love
for technology,
and at the same time a
great hate for it

3. technology, flex

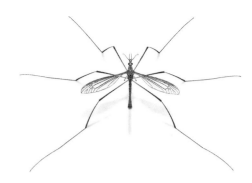

A great love because it is to industry that most of the benefits that we enjoy in this civilisation of ours must be attributed: it is in fact precisely its technology that enables us to look at the future with the hope of resolving the great problems of our world. It is always industry that favours major scientific innovations and it is always industry that gives us that extraordinary quality of life to which we are accustomed, providing us every day with a choice of products that has never been so huge.

At the same time I detest industry, because not only has it polluted the water of the seas and the air of the mountains, but it has also made the outskirts of our cities so ugly and has created an unprecedented gap between rich and poor; not only that, it has also standardised the world, homogenising products and making them commonplace, distancing us from the flavour of natural things, interposing the artificial.

ibility, transparency

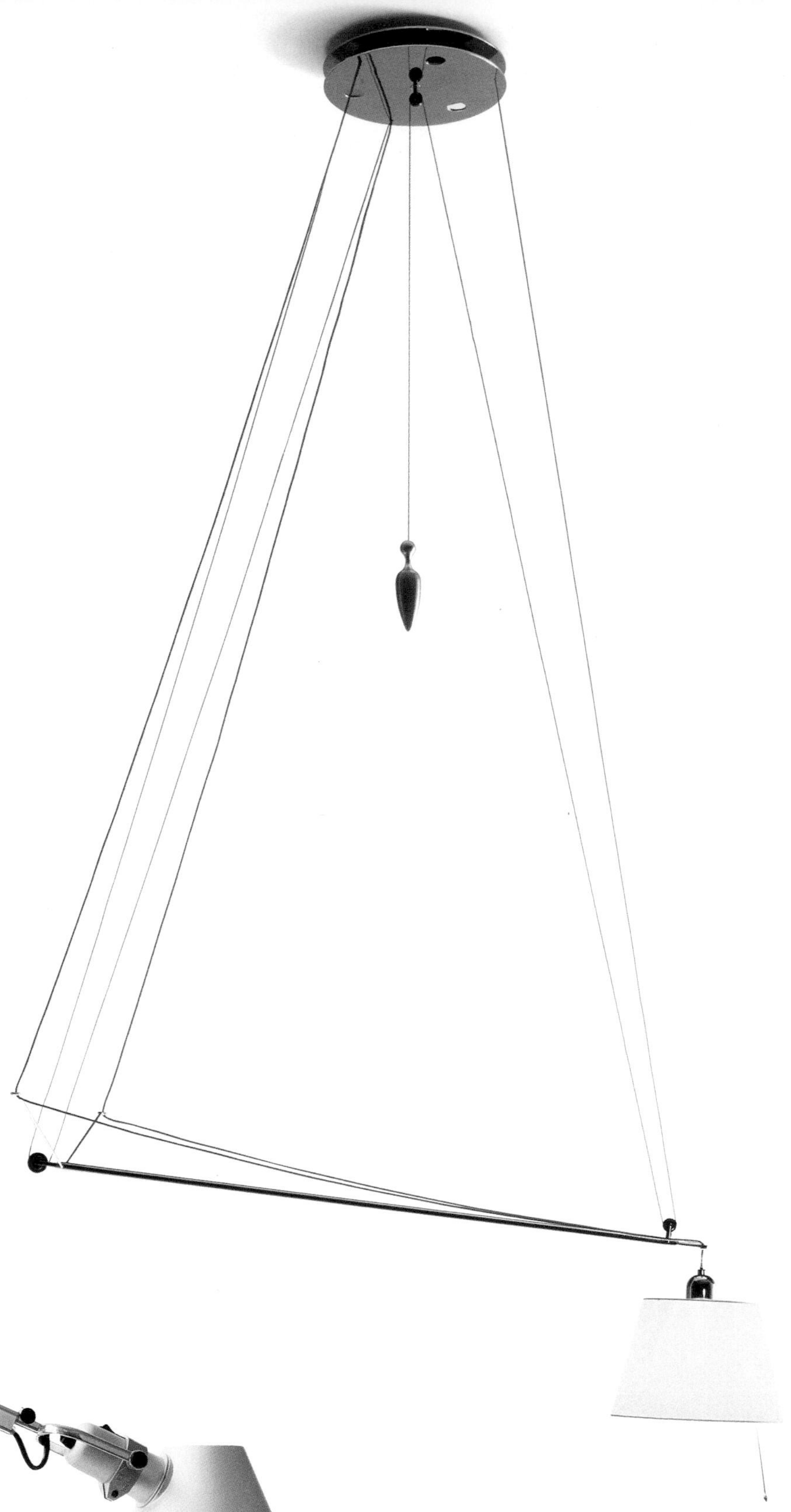

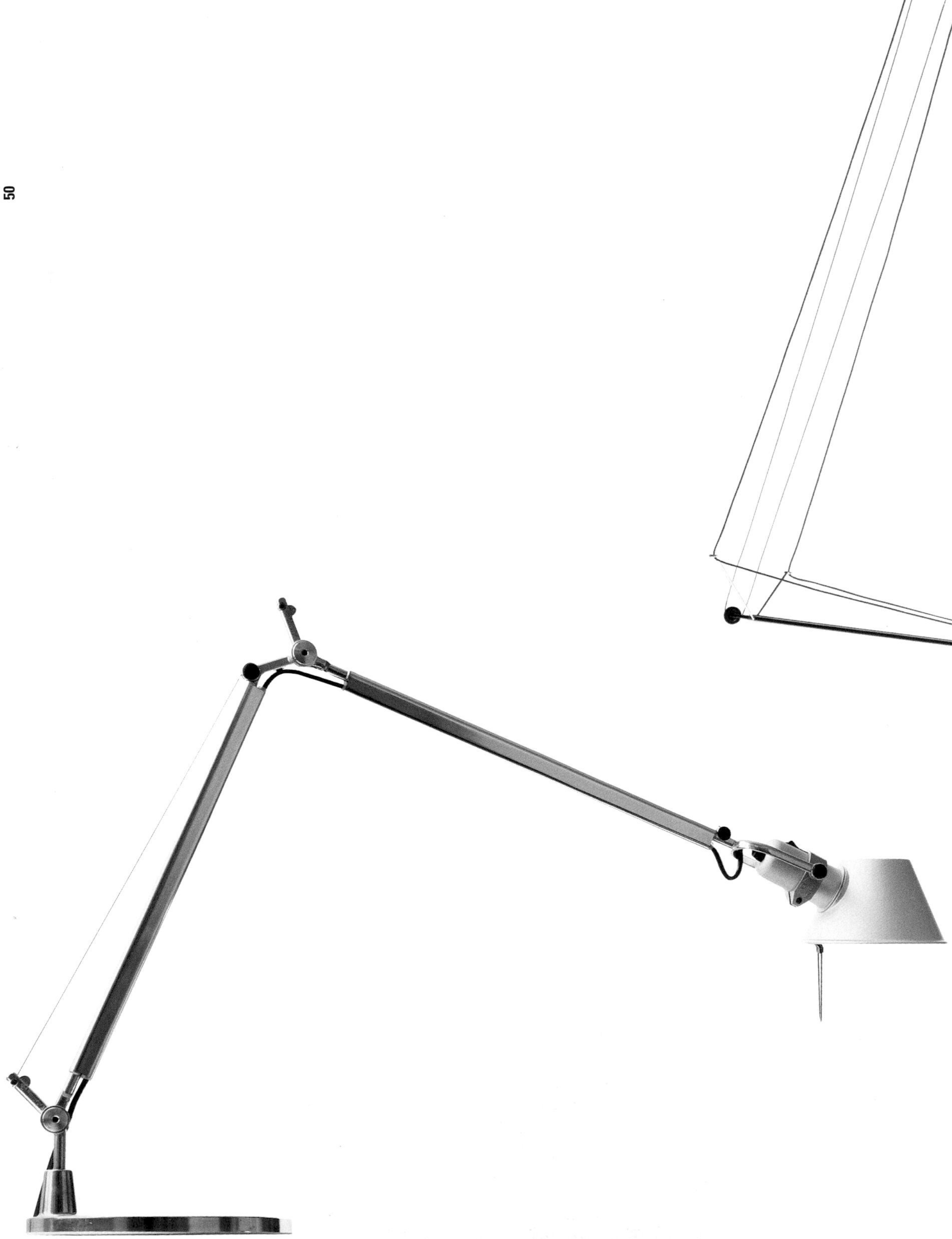

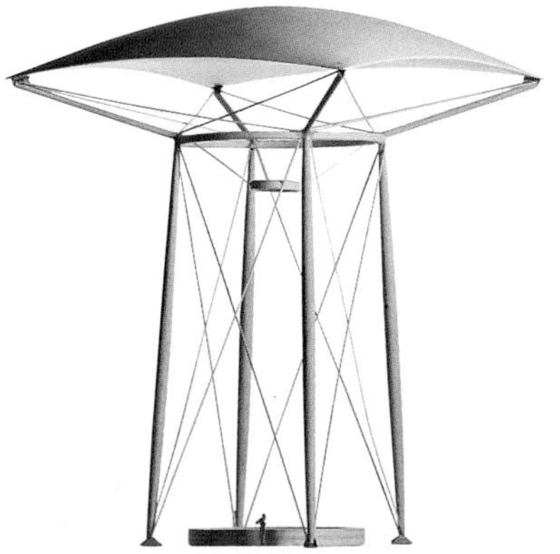

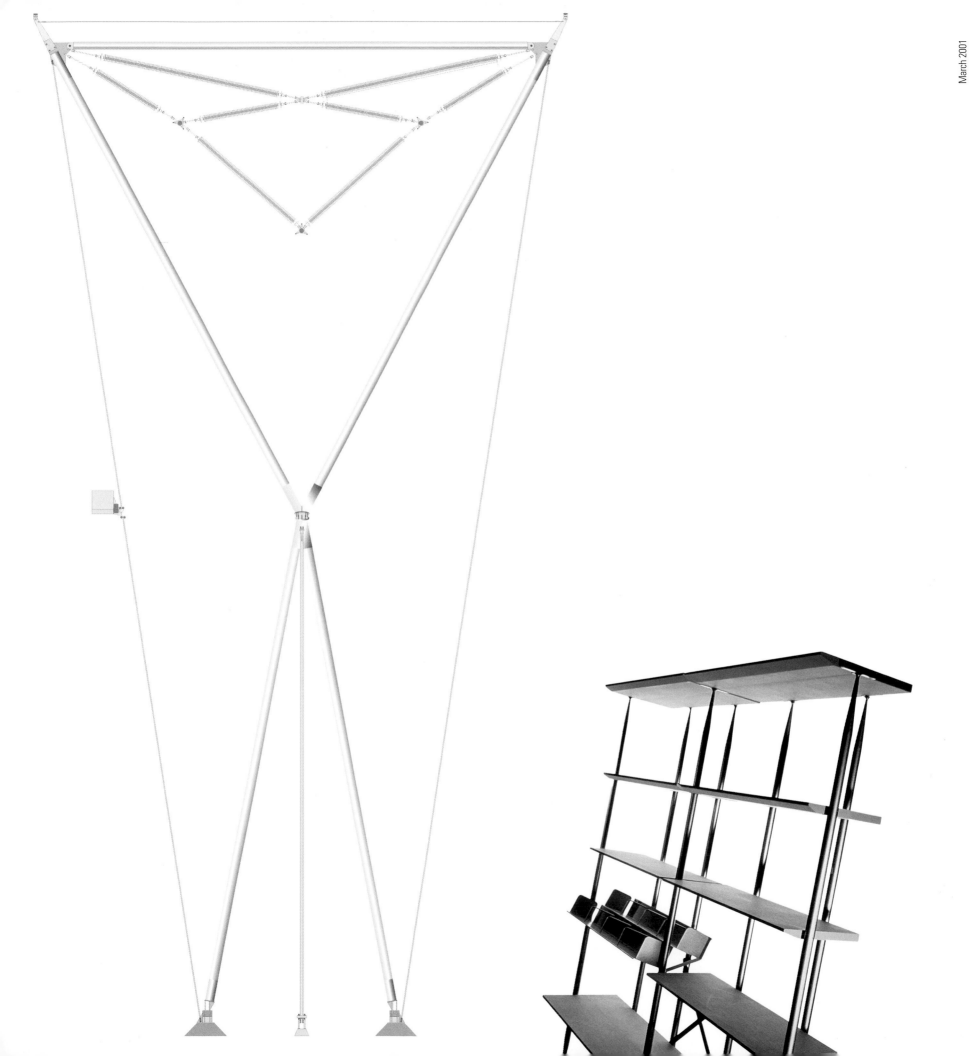

It is precisely in audacity that we fight the battle to define modernity

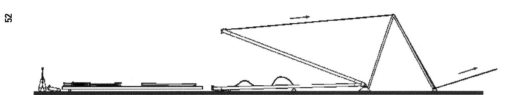

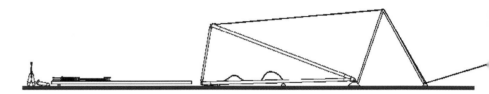

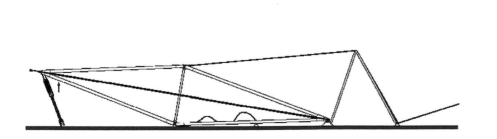

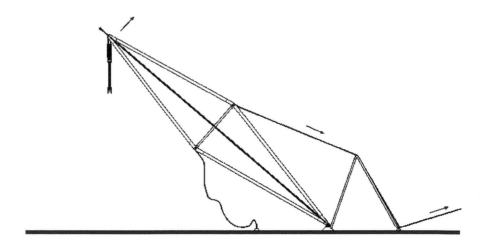

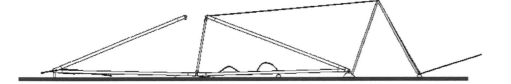

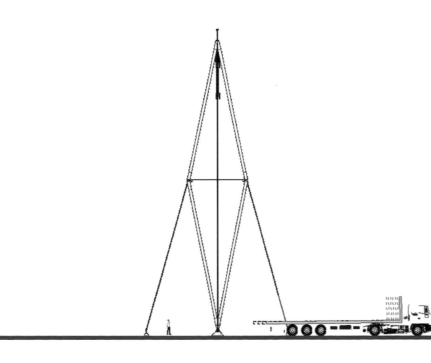

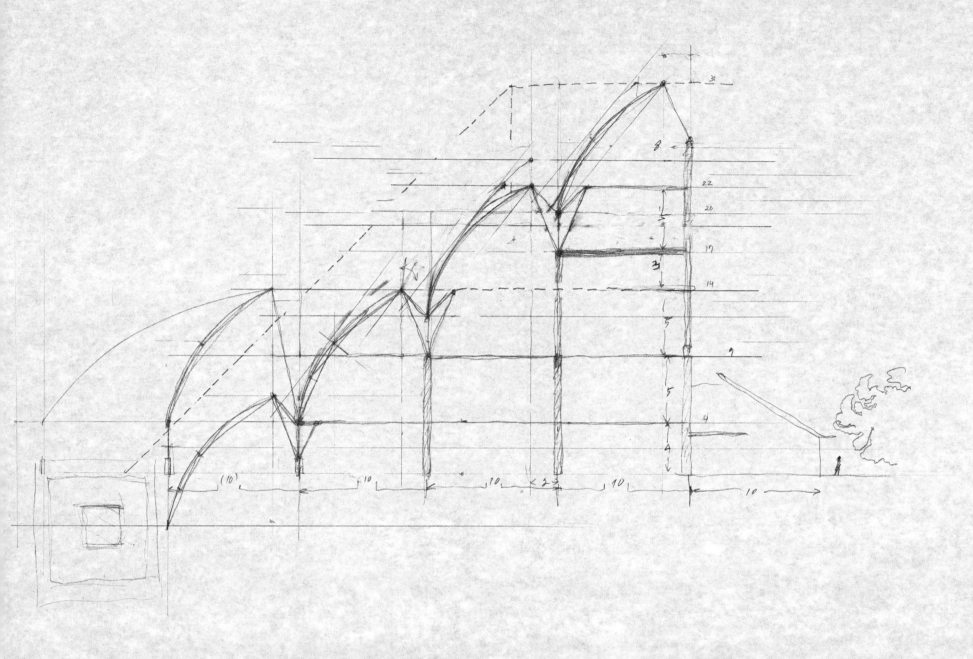

3·I
1999

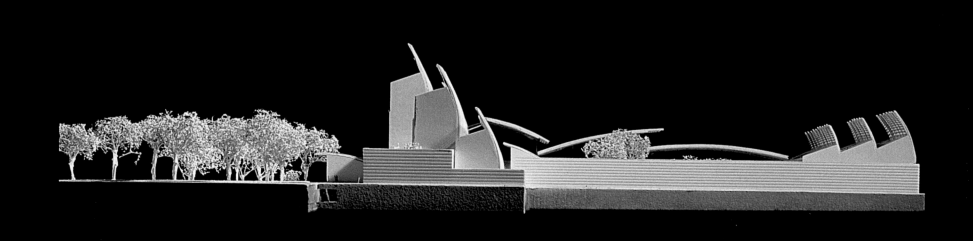

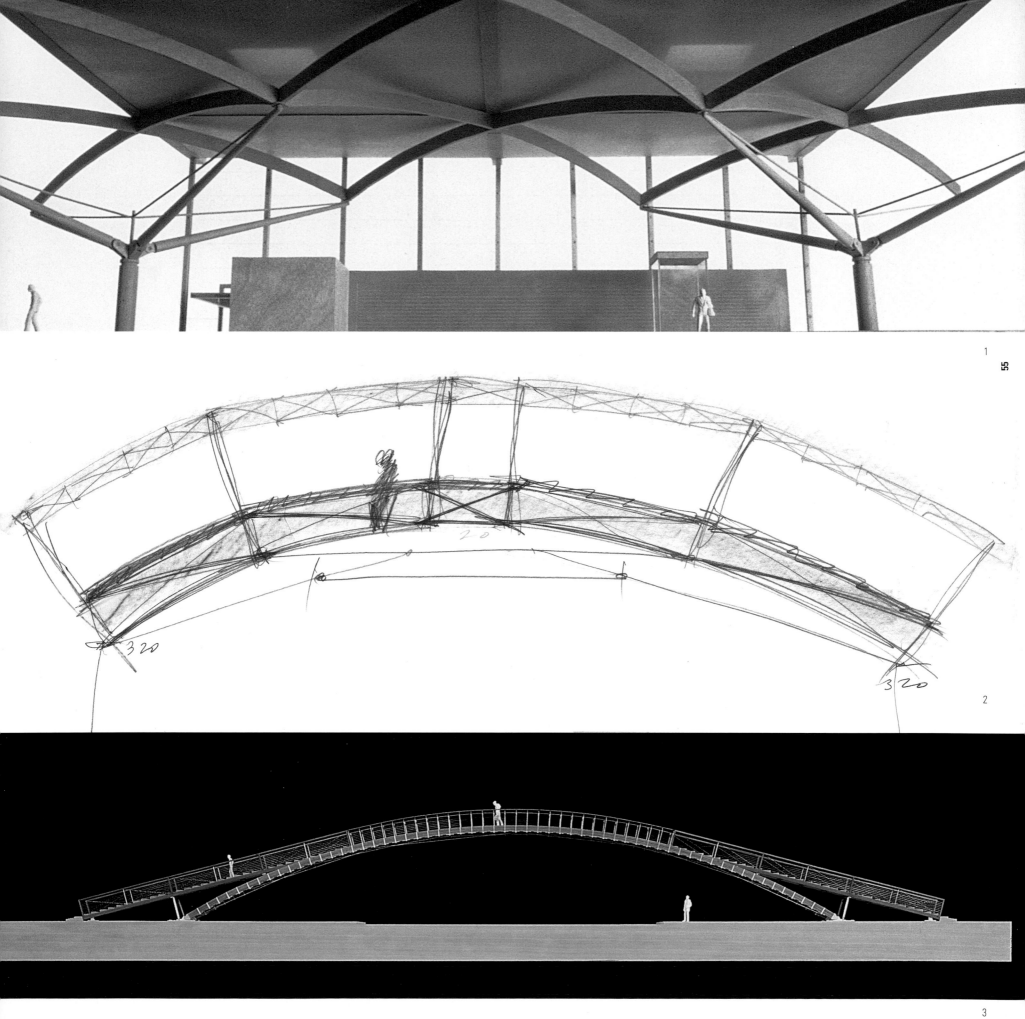

XII
1997

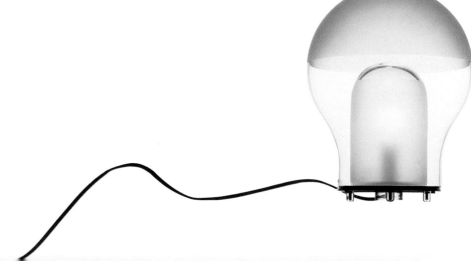

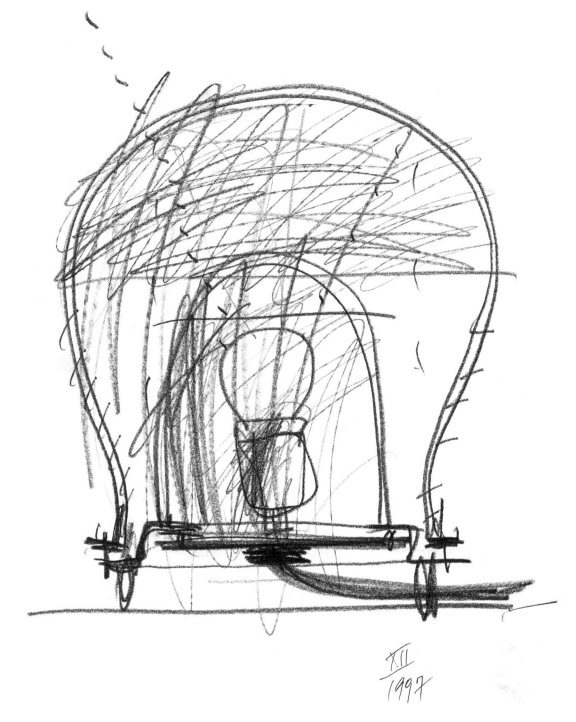

June 1998

I have called it Aria because this lamp has to do in some way with immateriality, intangibility, air.

The light source is invisible, masked by two overlapping glass caps, which filter the light through parts treated with satining and parts left transparent.

The glass of the caps is blown by master glass blowers of Murano and the whole lamp is made by Venetian craftsmen.

The form is vaguely reminiscent of a stylised light bulb, and is made abstract by the absence of the filament and the screw base.

Only the glass remains: the satining in the external cap masks the transparency of the internal cap, modulating the light with a little magic.

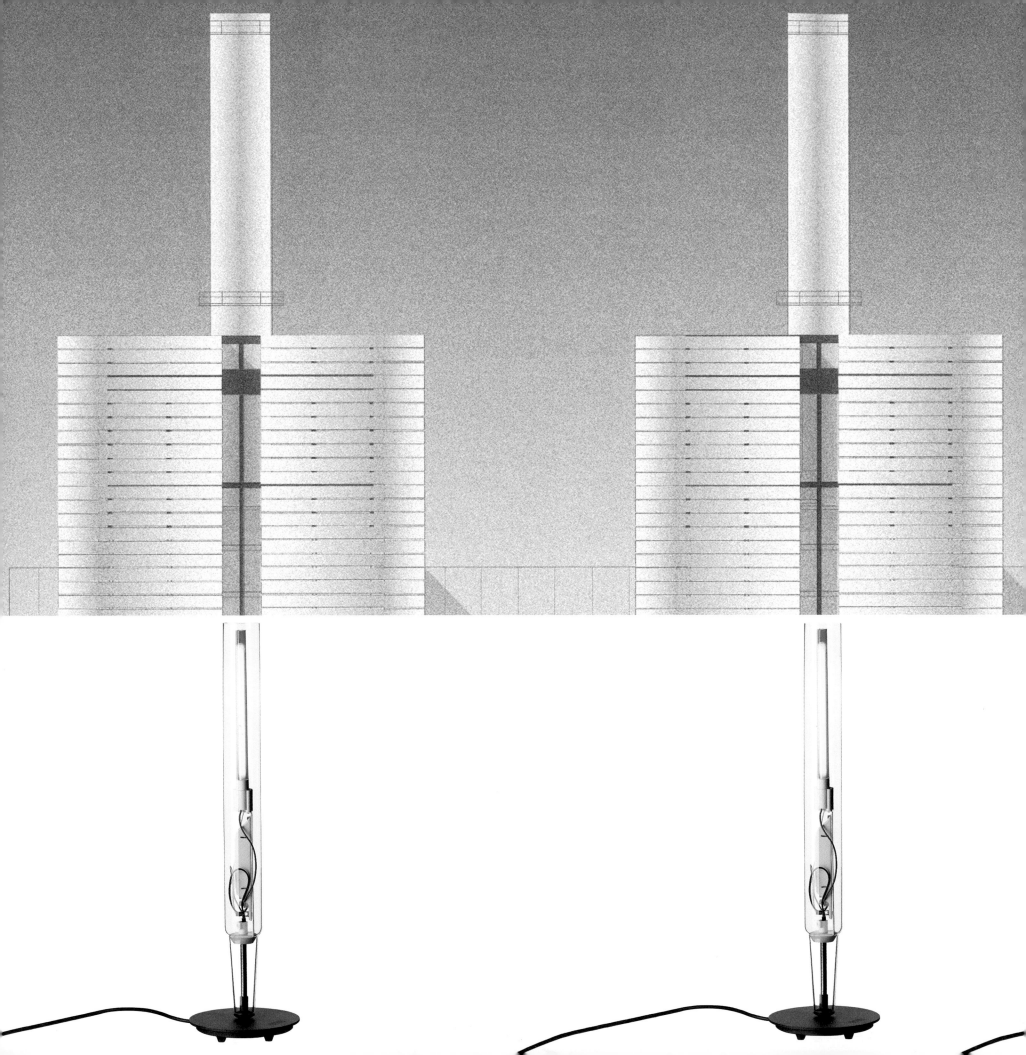

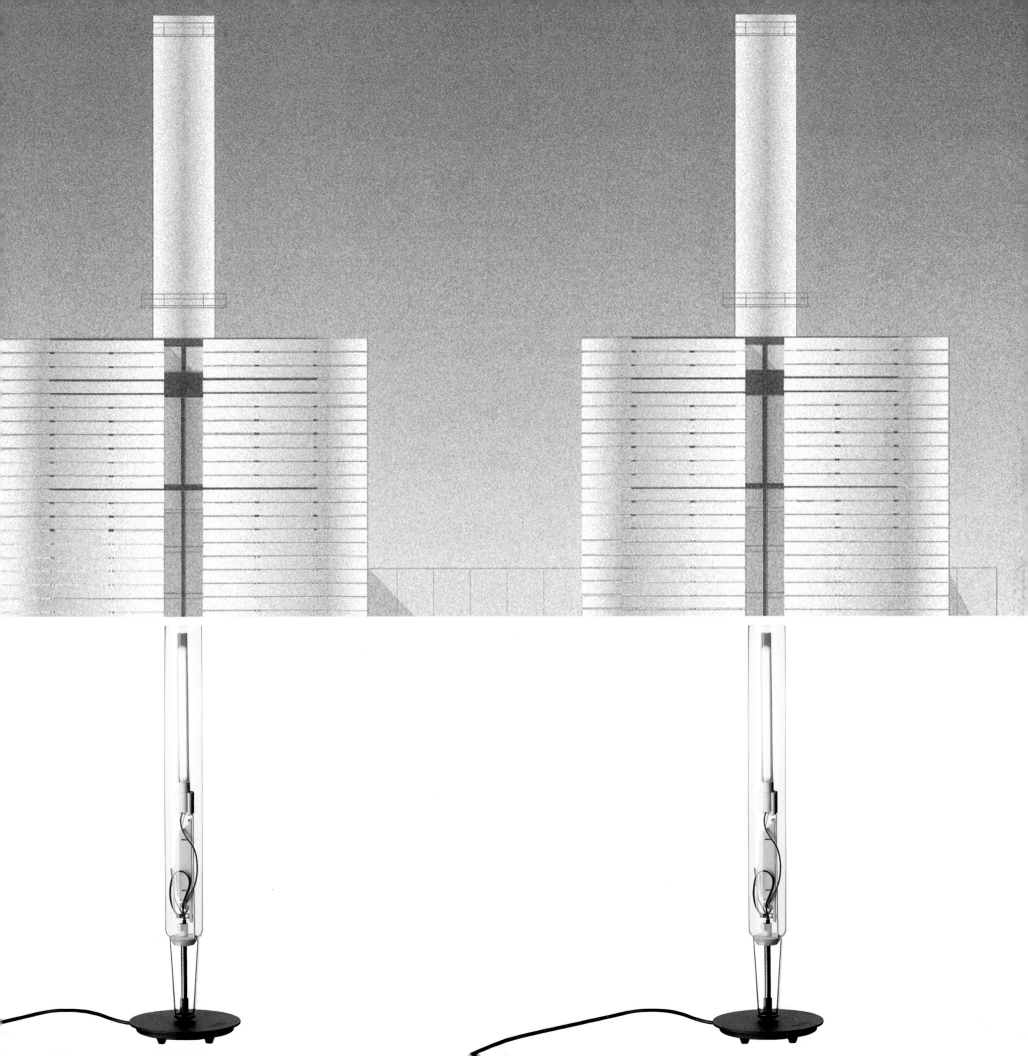

"a che cosa servono i vasi da fiori?" collection of vases

March 1999

… Is it so pathetic and out of fashion to make flowerpots?

… And so romantic and old-fashioned to devote yourself to composing flowers and leaves to make a decorative composition of them?

… And so manneristic and ephemeral?

Will it ever be meaningful to create vases of coloured glass with different forms, after people have been making vases for five hundred years?

… Today? Today, when everything has to be meaningful?

… When everything has to be worth something?

When everything has to be convenient and practical?

… Today, when only rationality and technology win?

For me, yes.

collection of "sufi" lamps

April 2000

How can we write about light, a thing so great that because of its beauty is so close to the image of God?

How can we talk about something to which our very existence, our birth and our death are linked?

How can we talk about light, when everything would be darkness, and perhaps is, in the places of places and in the time of time?

How can we talk about something that, when it varies, takes on all the gradations of feelings?

About something that crosses time and space, to arrive where the human mind cannot arrive?

I cannot; I am too small and superficial and I do not have either the mental strength or the words to express a concept that makes me dizzy at the mere thought of it; the source of light lies in darkness, where life has its origin.

In Sufi philosophy light has the same texture as the spirit; I can only, barely, understand that it is a thing so precious, so delicate, so high that it must be treated as the most sacred and transcendent thing that as humans we can perceive.

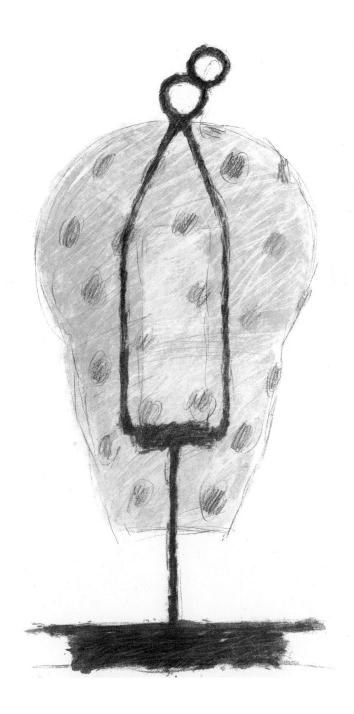

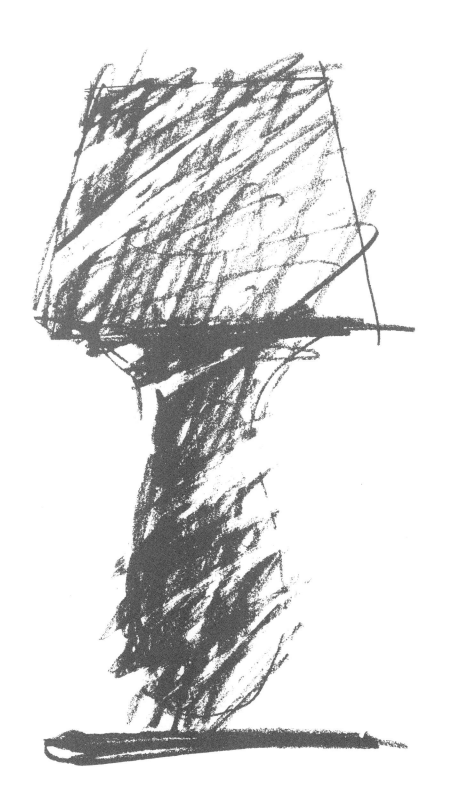

4. forms, curves,

March 2000

Getting straight to the point is a recognised quality of decisive and persevering people, and I would like to be like that too, but I am not

too I would like to draw straight and precise lines and signs, as though done with a ruler or on the computer, but I am not always

successful at it. So I often get round the problem. In reality everything is round and rounded and fluid forms are more sensual and suited to people, to their bodies and their environment: today the

computer and the most up-to-date production tools give us curves that were unthinkable a few years ago. The important thing is to be aware that under it all there is always old, mistreated, dear, sweet, beloved geometry.

fluidity

always successful at it. Rather, to avoid some problem or other, I often go round it. In design

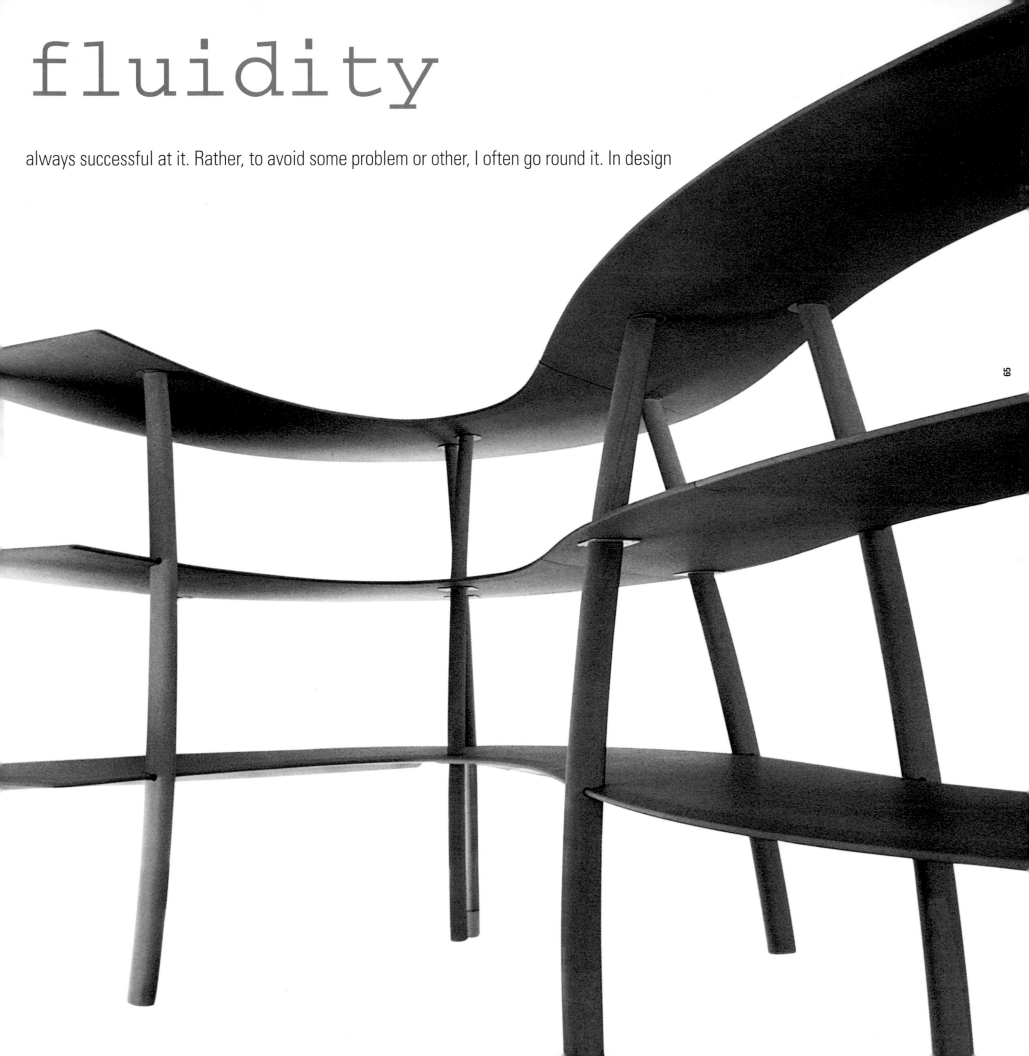

IN RECENT YEARS WE HAVE BECOME USED TO RECOGNISING ROUNDED AND SINUOUS FORMS AS MODERN AND TO REJECT RIGID AND ANGULAR FORMS AS OLD: WE STILL RECOGNISE, FOR EXAMPLE, ADVANCED SOLU-

TIONS AS EXPRESSLY INTEGRATED ELEMENTS, RATHER THAN SEPARATE AND DESIGNED INDEPENDENTLY. KNOWING HOW TO DISCOVER THESE CONCEPTS AND KNOWING HOW TO VARY THEM IN FORMS IS WHAT I HAVE

LEARNED IN RECENT YEARS AND I BELIEVE THAT THIS BEST EXPRESSES THE SENSE OF THE DESIGNER'S ACTIVITY IN INDUSTRY TODAY. DESIGNING DOES NOT MEAN SCULPTING OBJECTS, BUT ABOVE ALL GIVING THEM A

MEANING, FROM BOTH THE COMMUNICATIVE AND THE FUNCTIONAL AND ERGONOMIC STANDPOINTS. WE MUST NOT FORGET, IN FACT, THAT WE LIVE IN AN AGE WHEN INDUSTRY, THOUGH IT GIVES US SO MUCH, IS

UNDER INDICTMENT: INDUSTRIAL PRODUCTS HAVE ACQUIRED A MATURITY THE VALUE OF WHICH IS PONDERED UPON CONSIDERABLY BY CONTEMPORARY SOCIETY. THIS IS PRECISELY THE ROLE THAT ADRIANO OLIVETTI

ATTRIBUTED TO DESIGN: TO CONCEIVE QUALITY AND KNOW HOW TO EXPRESS IT.

soft   shades

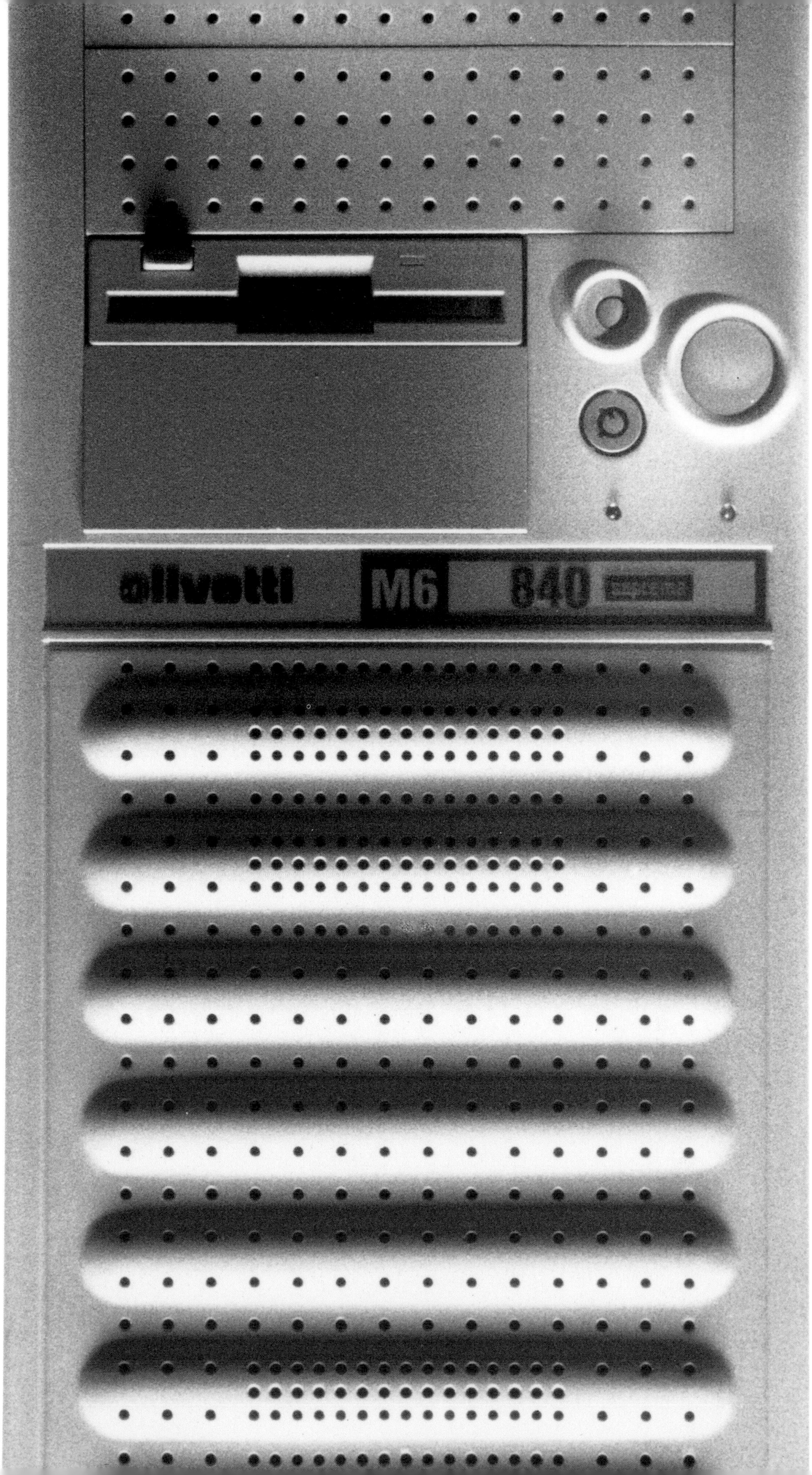
olivetti
M6
840

January 2002

THIS IS NOT A HOUSE WALL BUT IT IS A BOUNDARY WALL, A WALL IN THE OPEN AIR, A GARDEN WALL … A WALL THAT,

LIKE ALL WALLS IN THE OPEN AIR IN THE COUNTRY, STOPS AT A CERTAIN HEIGHT AND YOU APPRECIATE IT FOR ITS

PROPORTIONS AND ITS MATERIAL NATURE, BUT IT IS NOT MADE TO SUPPORT A FLOOR … IT IS A WALL THAT IS REM-

INISCENT OF THE JAPANESE WALL AND NOT THE SUPPORT FOR A BUILDING. EVEN THE DOOR THAT IS MADE IN THE

WALL IS NOT THE DOOR OF A FLAT, BUT IS THE PORTAL OF AN EMPEROR'S PALACE.

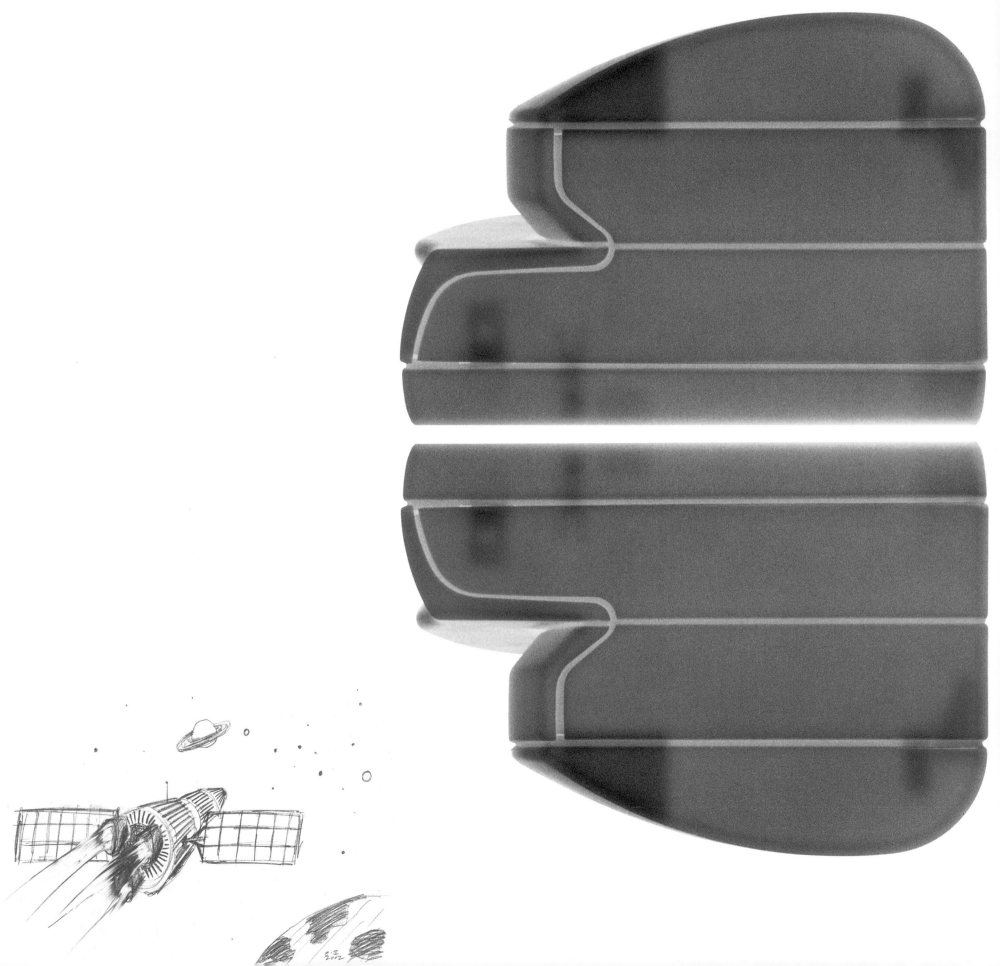

Form as movement,
as action,
active form is good.
Form as rest,
as end, is bad.
Passive, finished
form is bad.
Formation is good,
form is bad;
form is the end, death.
Formation is movement, act.
Formation is life.

Paul Klee

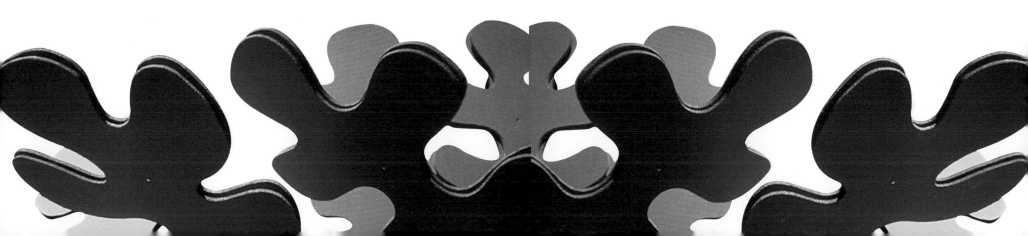

Artfer 70

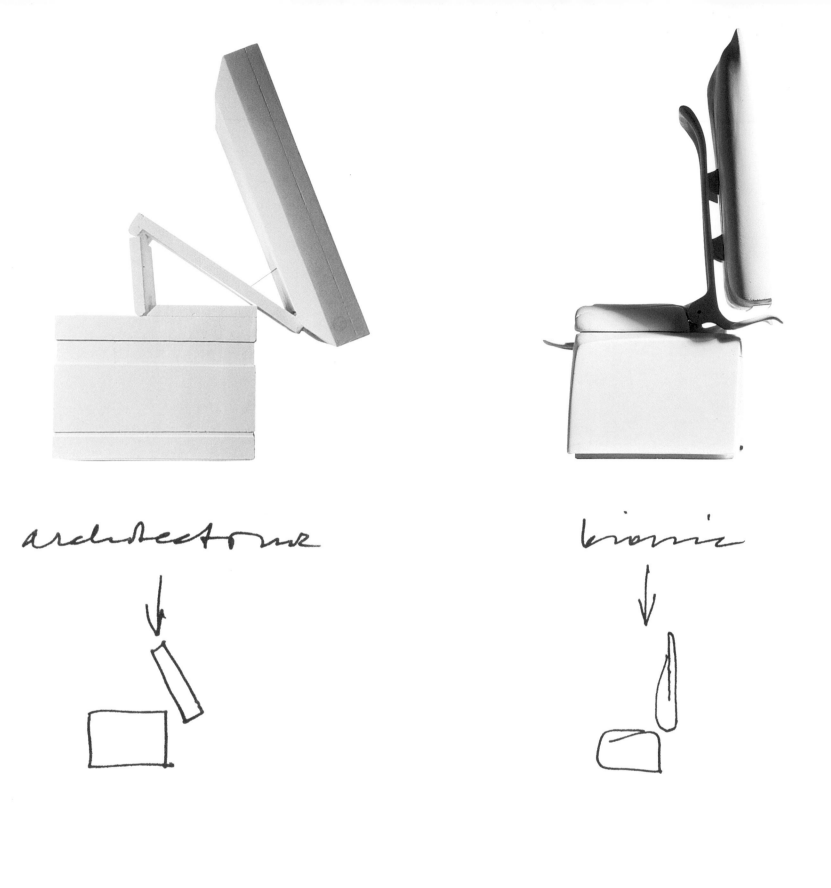

architectonic

bionic

sculpture

organic

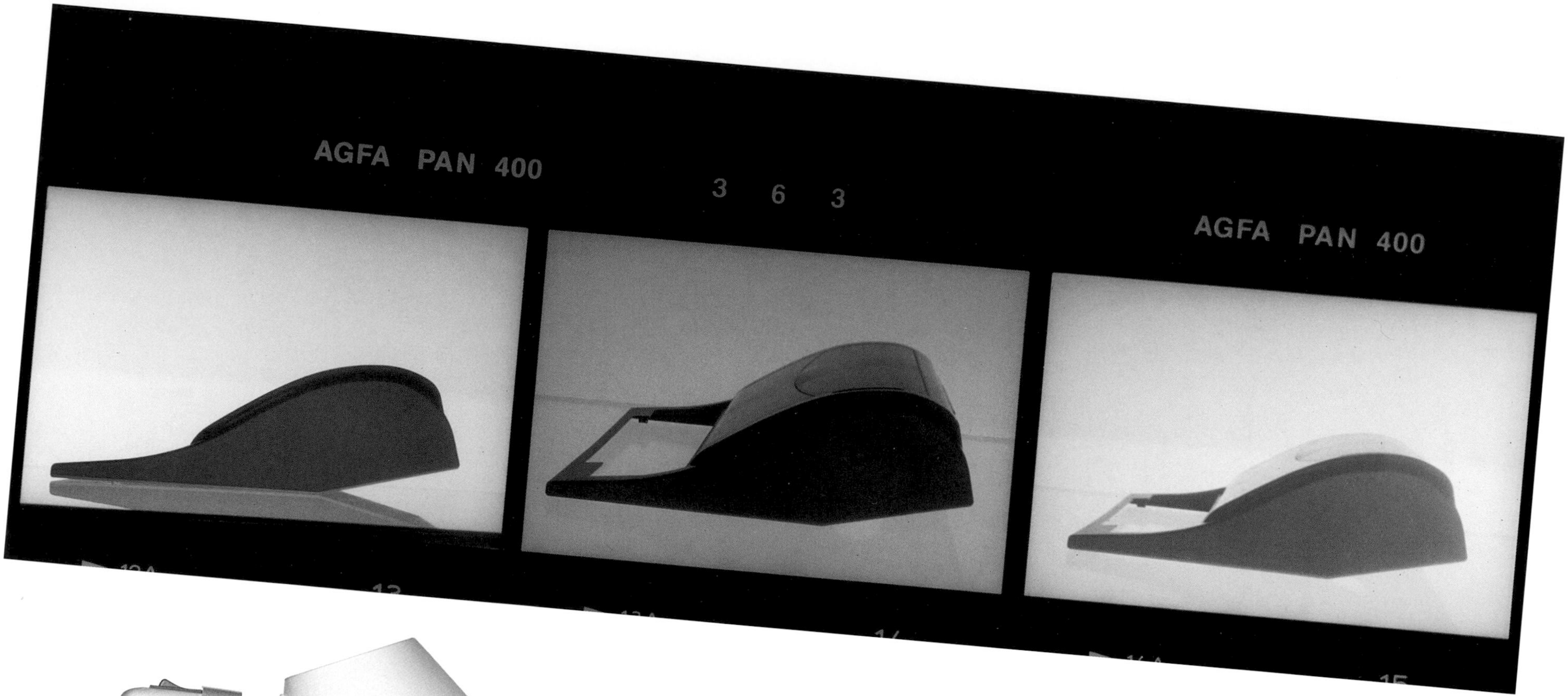
AGFA PAN 400
3 6 3
AGFA PAN 400

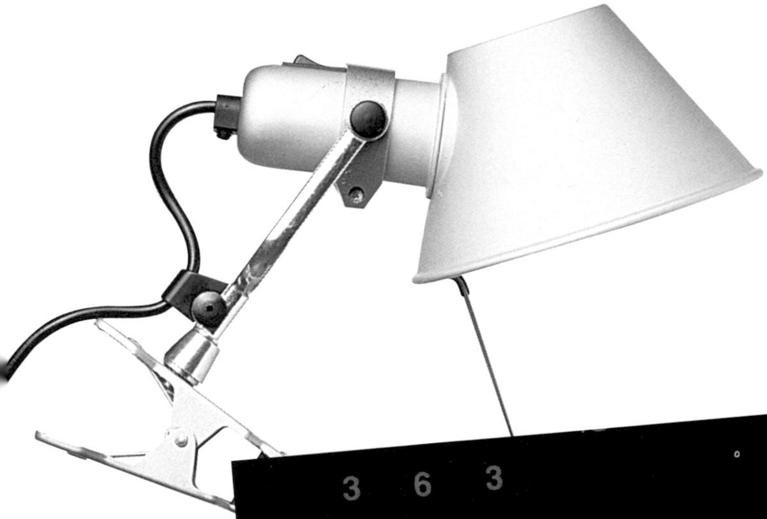

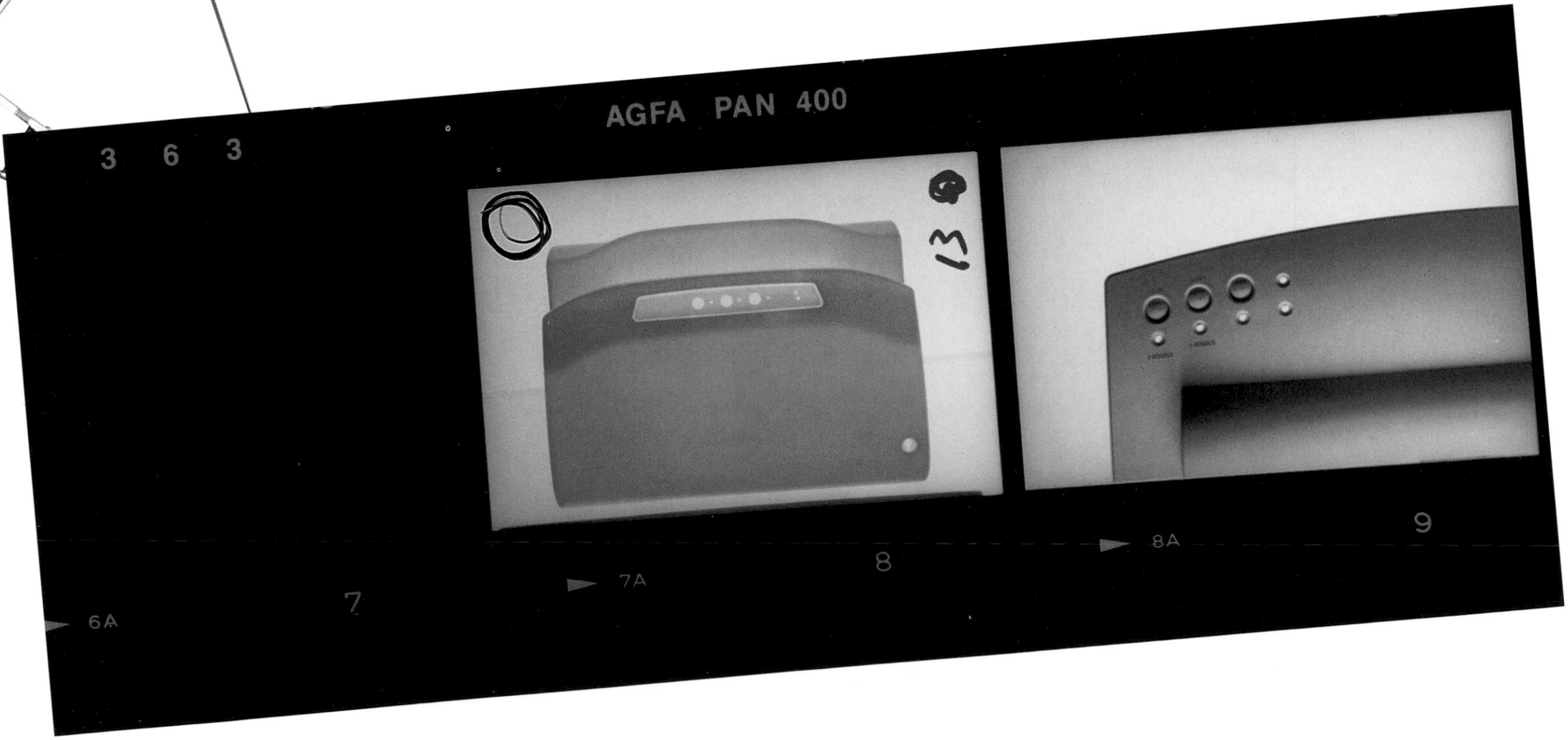
3 6 3
AGFA PAN 400
13
9
8A
8
7A
7
6A

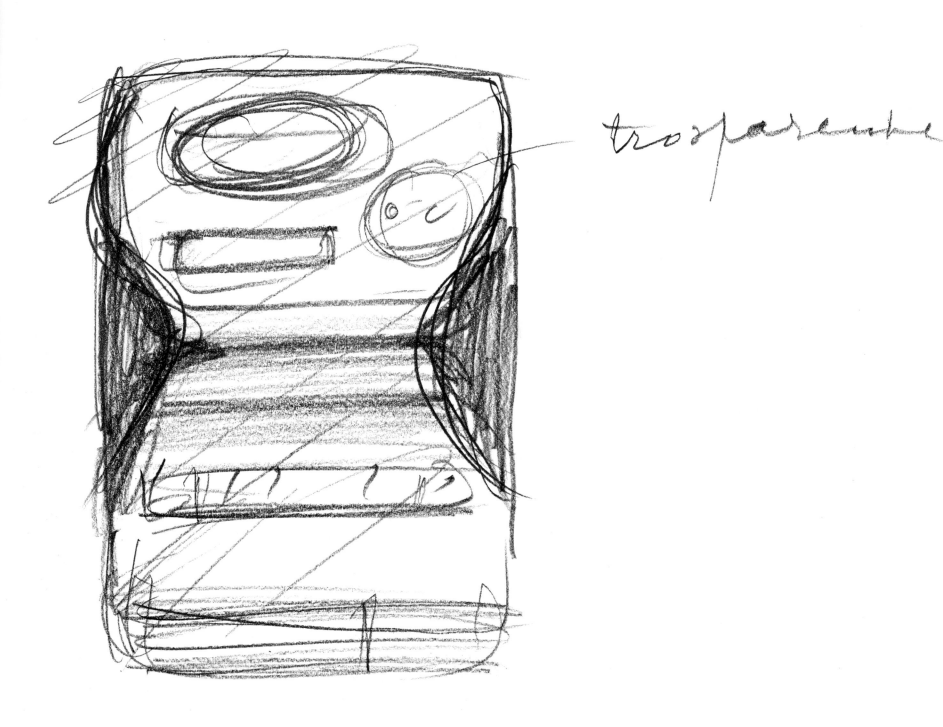

trasparente

June 1997

MASS PRODUCTION IS NOT SIMPLY KNOWING
but it is knowing how to position
it well throughout ITS

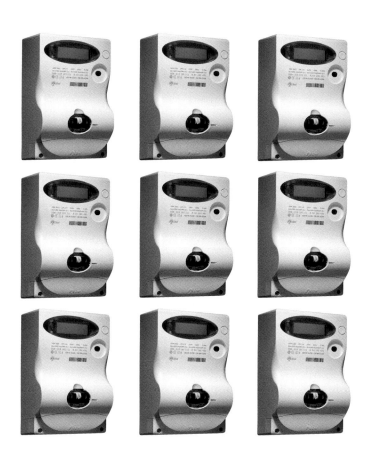

HOW TO MAKE A PRODUCT MANY TIMES,

LIFE

MY RELATIONSHIP WITH OLIVETTI IS CERTAINLY ALSO A VERY EMOTIONAL RELATIONSHIP. WHEN ETTORE SOTTSASS

FOUND ME A JOB WITH OLIVETTI FOR THE FIRST TIME, I WAS SO EXCITED AND BECAME SO INVOLVED IN THAT JOB

THAT IMMEDIATELY, FROM THE VERY FIRST MOMENT, I MADE IT THE MOST IMPORTANT POSITION IN MY PROFESSION-

AL LIFE. OVER THE YEARS OLIVETTI HAS GIVEN MORE AND MORE; IT HAS BEEN A SCHOOL OF DESIGN AND EXTRAORDI-

NARY LIFE. IT IS DIFFERENT FROM THE OTHER COMPANIES FOR WHICH I HAVE WORKED, PRECISELY ON ACCOUNT OF

THIS CONTINUITY WITH WHICH I HAVE BEEN ABLE TO FOLLOW THE EVOLUTION OF THE PRODUCTS, THE MENTALITY OF

THE PEOPLE, AND IT IS DIFFERENT FROM THE OTHER COMPANIES BECAUSE IT DEALS WITH AN EXTRAORDINARY

THEME, WHICH IS THE THEME OF TECHNOLOGY. AS I SAID, I AM CONVINCED THAT TODAY THE REASONS WHY WE FEEL

GOOD OR BAD ARE ALL LINKED TO TECHNOLOGY, SO DEALING WITH THE PROJECT OF TECHNOLOGY MEANS DEALING

WITH THE THEME OF THE PROJECT FOR MANKIND'S FUTURE AND DESIGNING MANKIND'S FUTURE IS THE REASON WHY

I AM HAPPY TO BE AN ARCHITECT TODAY.

17 June 1997

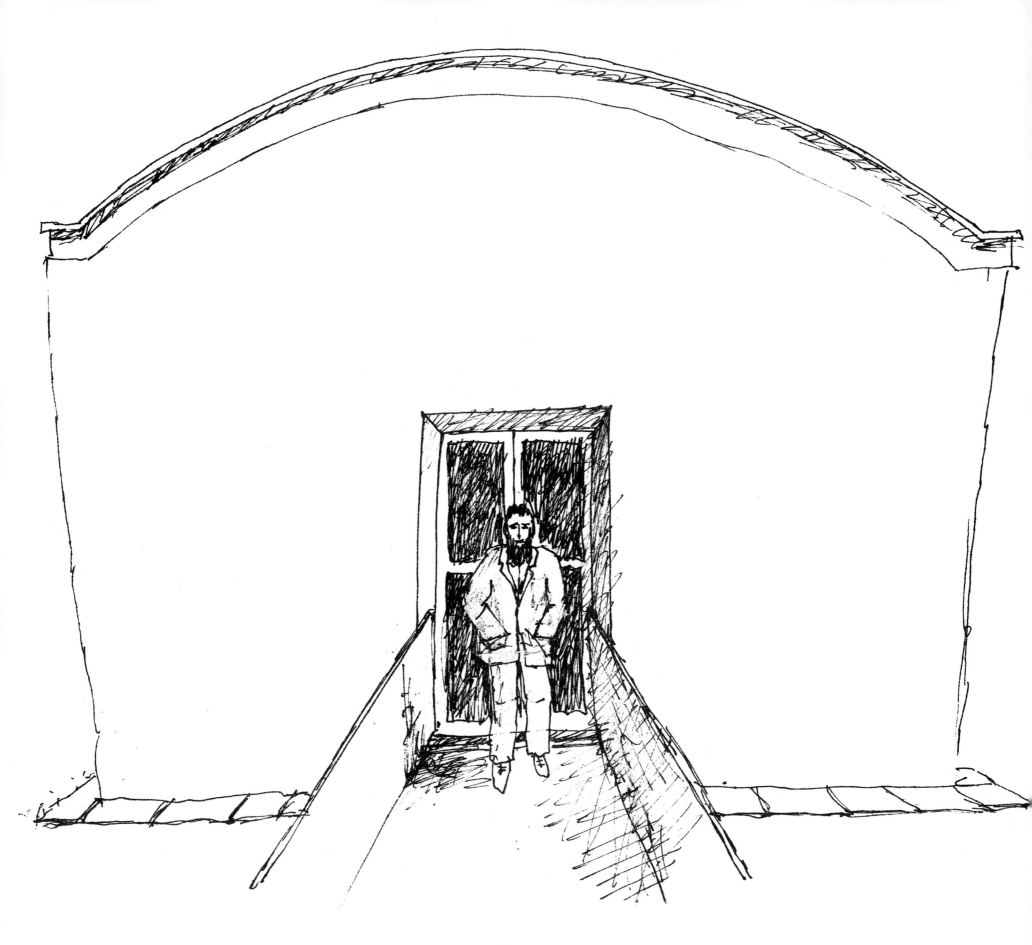

5. memories, paran

August 2001, lithograph

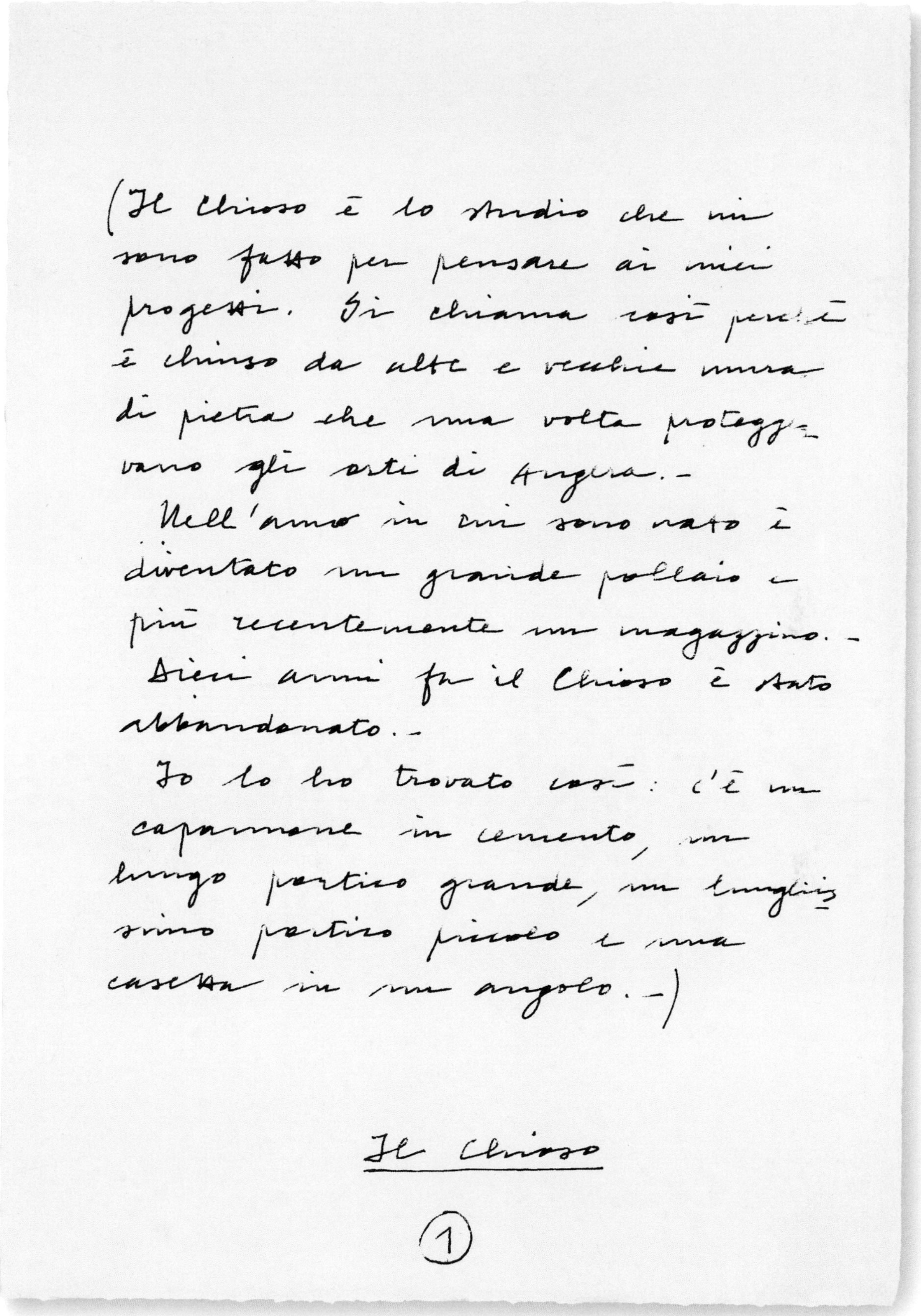

(Il Chiosso è lo studio che mi sono fatto per pensare ai miei progetti. Si chiama così perché è chiuso da alte e vecchie mura di pietra che una volta proteggevano gli orti di Angera. –

Nell'anno in cui sono nato è diventato un grande pollaio e più recentemente un magazzino. –

Dieci anni fa il Chiosso è stato abbandonato. –

Io lo ho trovato così: c'è un capannone in cemento, un lungo portico grande, un lunghissimo portico piccolo e una casetta in un angolo. –)

Il Chiosso

①

oias, absurdities

Chioso

The Cloister

All the buildings are constructed along the boundary walls and all face onto a large central lawn, so it is all very protected and you almost seem to be in a monastery cloister.

The Gate

You enter the Chioso through an old iron gate, which is right in the corner of the walls. From outside the walls are very high and serve as a crown for the large oak trees, the nut trees, the cypresses, the camellias.

The Studio

The studio is a long shed with seven large windows; inside it is a single large space with a raised floor and a long curved wall that conceals the archive.

I have planted eight cypresses in front.

The Large Portico

The large portico has twelve cement columns, French gutter roof tiles and a single long back wall.

Inside I have put the workshop, the store and the garage. There is also an archive and accommodation.

The Small Portico

The small portico has thirty-two columns and runs along all the boundary walls towards the Rocca [Fortress]. It is very long and beautiful and I use it for walks and do not get lost when I am deep in thought.

The Garden of Camellias

Slightly raised, behind the studio, is the garden of camellias: they are all rare, collection plants, placed in line along a path, in this sunny, sheltered corner.

The Bamboo Room

The Chioso has an open corner, between the studio and the large portico. There is a small square here, paved with large stones and a magnolia growing in the middle. A bamboo curtain closes it inside a room that has the sky for a roof.

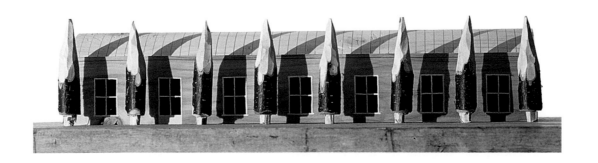

THE LITTLE COTTAGE IN THE WOOD. IN THE OUTSIDE CORNER THERE IS A MYSTERIOUS COTTAGE THAT WAS ONCE USED FOR SHELTER AND TO PUT AWAY THE TOOLS. I SOMETIMES SLEEP THERE, NOT ALONE.

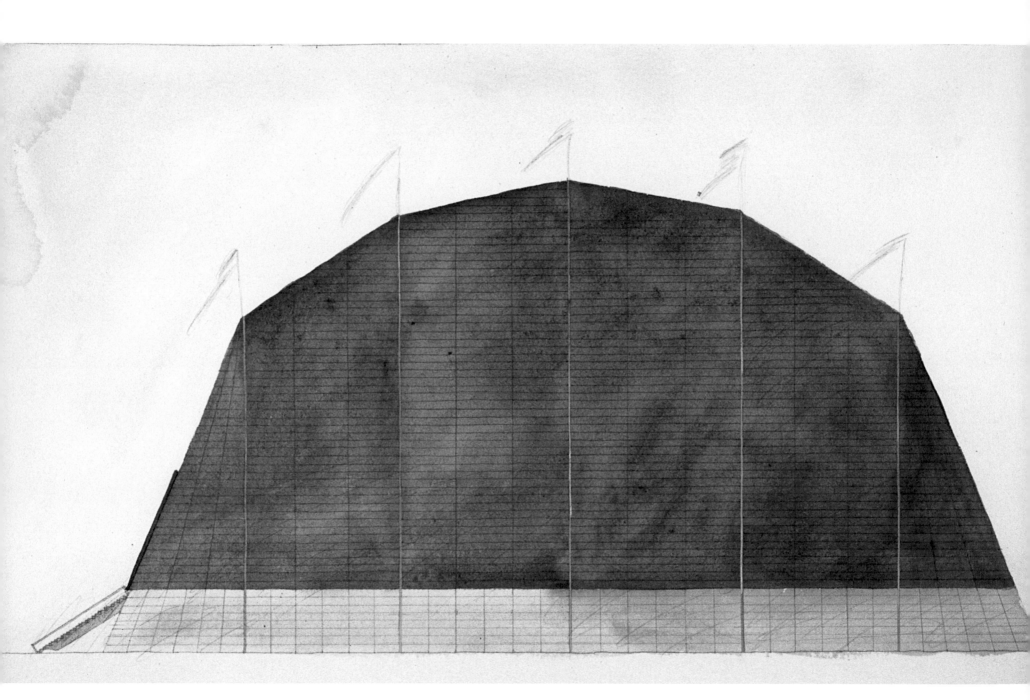

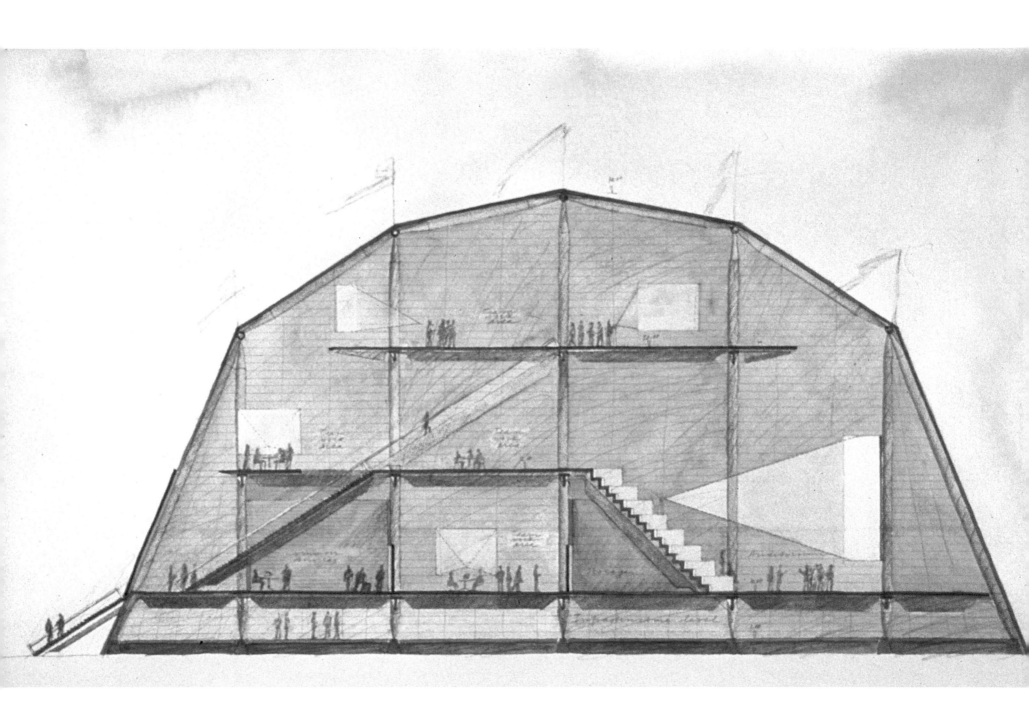

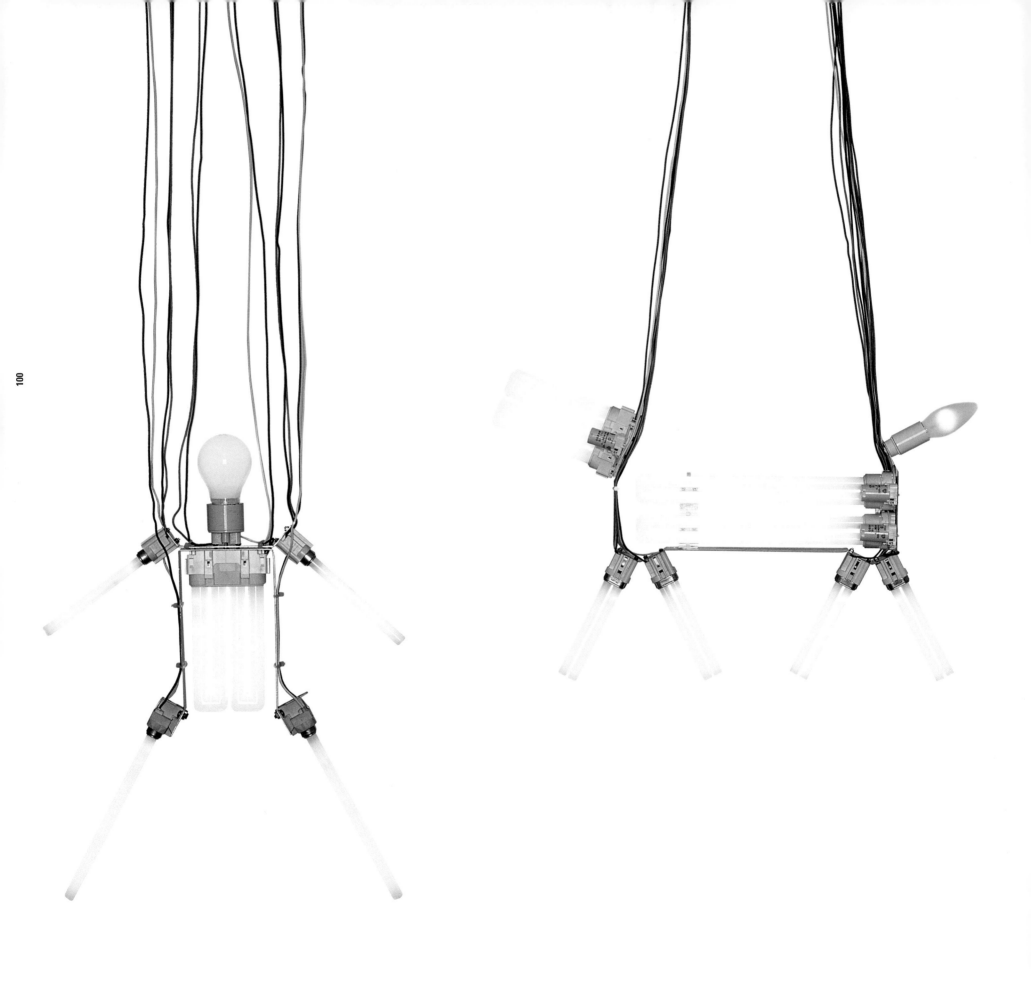

A PUPPET, A DOG, A FACE. A GAME, A SPELL, A TRICK. THESE ARE LAMPS ENDOWED WITH A SOUL THAT IS PERCEIVED WHEN, SUSPENDED FROM THE CEILING AND TURNED OFF,

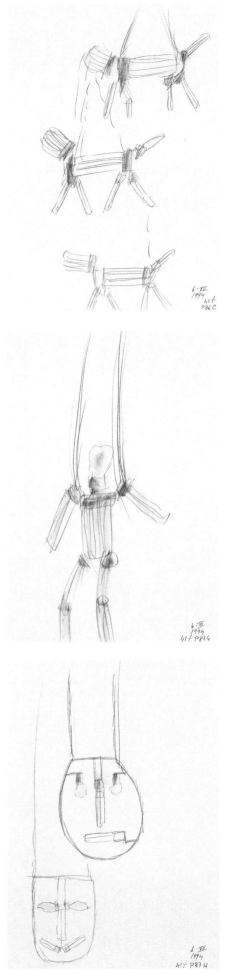

THEY SEEM TO WAIT IN THE DARKNESS TO THEN, WHEN TURNED ON, WAKE UP AGAIN AND LIVE THEIR OWN LIVES.

Produzione privata esiste
segretamente già da
qualche anno ed è
come dire da il nome
stesso. La produzione
privata e personale di
un architetto che vuole
avere una parte della
sua attività e della
sua anima più ~~segreta~~
~~e personale~~ apportata –
Con queste cose non
si propone di sorprender
nessuno ne tanto meno
far arrabbiare alcuno,
ma delle vere
ragioni che lo ha opini

18 October 1990, notebook no. 10

Trabiccolo

I have always thought that an ideal place to surf on the Internet, as we do today, does not exist. I do so in my studio with the computer that I have behind me, I do so at home in the walk-in wardrobe, where we have put the home computer, I do so on Franco's computer, because it is faster, and sometimes somewhere in the office, on the first computer I find free. But I have not yet found a truly beautiful place to hide away, to keep calm, with no pressure, no stress, without the urgent need to deliver projects the following day.

To use the computer comfortably, the best position is to sit back slightly, because it is like going to the cinema and the monitor has to be large and luminous and positioned with adjustable height. The table must be very movable, adjustable and fixable in any position with a simple hand movement. It must be able to rest on the knees, to have keyboard and mouse in the most comfortable position. It has to be a small room, full of comfort, not too bright, not too dark.

So when I was invited to design what I wanted, provided it was made of wood, the first thing I thought of was a boat,
because I have never had one and this could be an opportunity. Then I thought that a caravan was more urgently needed, to solve my problem of an Internet place,
and so I came up with a carriage that is in many ways a boat, and I called it Trabiccolo.
It is a carriage because I would like to take it around with me, I do not know where yet, but to a beautiful place. Because it is good to use the beautiful places
in the world, but I do not want to ruin them and if we all go there with caravans, then they become a huge parking lot of plastic boxes with big glass doors and windows.
At least my carriage is all made of American wood, solid and polished, and the glass doors and windows are small.
It would be so beautiful if it could also float, but I envisage some modifications.

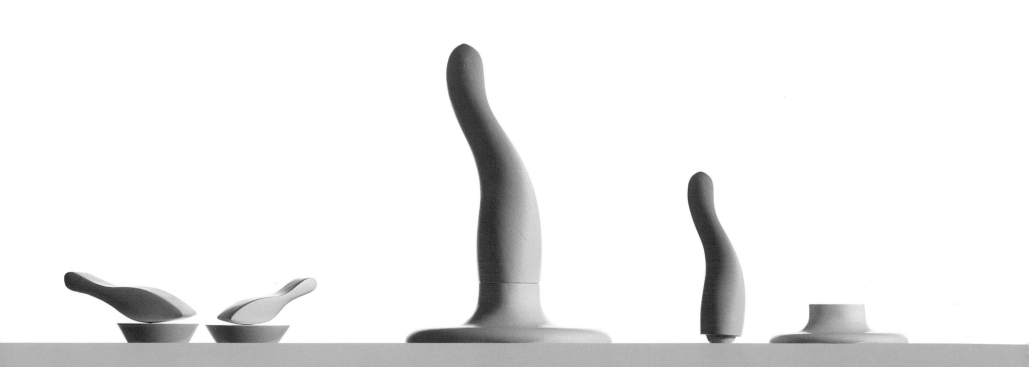

La Cerbaia
Estate 1987

Building a table means founding a house. The table is the very model of the house, of work, of human relations, around which the architecture is built…

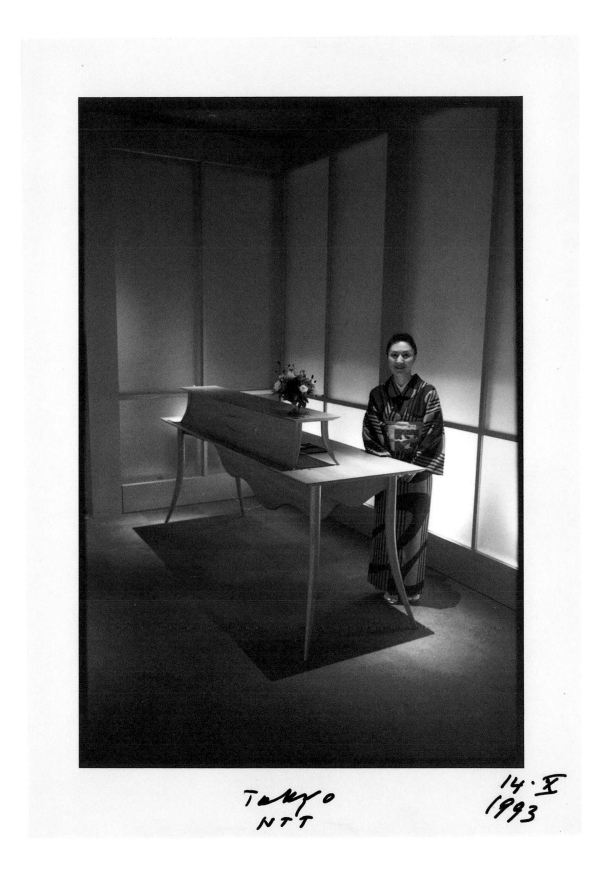

TOKYO
NTT

14·X
1993

... The city is in fact a set of tables, that is, a set of charismatic centres around which people gather. Andrea Branzi

April 2001

I AM STILL CONVINCED THAT WE LIVE IN A ROMANTIC AGE. THE MORE CONSUMERISM GOES ON, THE MORE NEED OF ROMANTICISM WE HAVE. TODAY EVERYTHING IS MADE TO STRIKE YOUR SENSES, AND THIS IS THE PURE MATRIX OF ROMANTICISM. TODAY YOU NEED TO EXCITE.

Piazza di Spagna

IT IS A PROJECT OF INTUITION, DIFFERENT FROM A PROJECT OF COMPOSITION, WHERE HARMONY AND INNOVATION ARE COMPOSED TO GIVE FORM TO A NEW OBJECT.

THIS IS AN OLD PROJECT FOR A NEW, VERY NEW PRODUCT, MUCH SUITED TO TODAY.

OUR SMALL DIVAN IN THE STYLE OF A BENCH IS CALLED PIAZZA DI SPAGNA (FROM THE ADDRESS OF THE OLIVETTI CORPORATE HEAD OFFICE IN ROME) AND IS THE MOST CONCRETE AND INTELLIGENT ALTERNATIVE TO THE BARE AND MINIMALIST COUCHES THAT INVADE THE SHOP WINDOWS OF FURNISHING SHOPS TODAY.

IT IS BOTH THE RICHEST AND THE MOST MODEST FURNISHING ELEMENT THAT CAN BE CONCEIVED TODAY, WITH ITS HUGE CACHET OF HISTORY, CULTURE AND TRADITION.

Merry Christmas and Happy Two Thousand

You see things; and you say 'Why?'
But I dream things that never were; and I say 'Why not?'

G. B. Shaw

Tu vedi cose che esistono e dici
'perché?'
Ma io sogno cose mai esistite
e dico
'perché no?'

L'eredità personale del Mahatma Gandhi
The personal heritage of Mahatma Gandhi

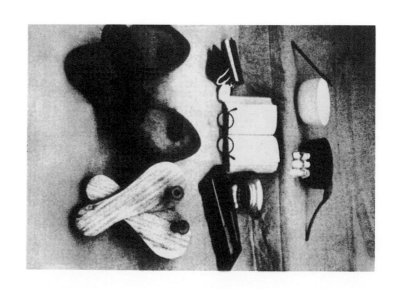

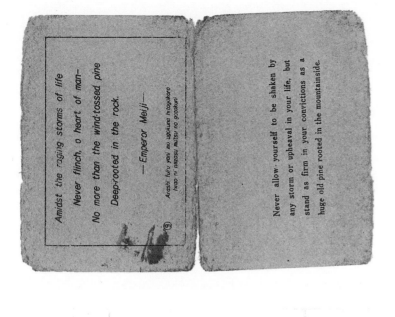

Amidst the raging storms of life

Never flinch, o heart of man—

No more than the wind-tossed pine

Deep-rooted in the rock.

—Emperor Meiji—

Arashi fuku yo no uzukuma hitogokoro
Iwao ni nezasu matsu no gotakuni

Never allow yourself to be shaken by any storm or upheaval in your life, but stand as firm in your convictions as a huge old pine rooted in the mountainside.

Non ti lasciar scuotere dalle burrasche della vita, cuore di uomo, ma rimani saldo nelle tue convinzioni così come un grande vecchio pino con le radici profonde nel roccioso pendio della montagna.
Imperatore Meiji

Albero in Giappone

...non sono solo la forma e la materia che fanno belle le cose...

...it is not only shape and material that make things beautiful...
Michele De Lucchi

..... in attesa del prossimo momento epico......

Michele De Lucchi was born in 1951 in Ferrara and graduated in Architecture in Florence. In the years of radical and experimental architecture, he was among the protagonists of movements such as Cavart, Alchymia and Memphis.

De Lucchi has designed products for Artemide, Dada Cucine, Kartell, Matsushita, Mauser, Poltrona Frau, Olivetti, for whom he has been Head of Design since 1992. He has devised various personal theories on the evolution of the working environment and has developed experimental projects for Compaq Computers, Philips, Siemens, Vitra. Above all he has designed buildings for offices, realised in Japan, Germany and Italy. Since 1999 he has been entrusted with the redevelopment of Enel Produzione's electricity plants.

Many of his interiors for services are in use by Deutsche Bank, Deutsche Bundesbahn, Enel, Poste Italiane, Telecom Italia, Banca Popolare di Lodi and other Italian and foreign institutes.

He has designed buildings for public and private museums. He has been responsible for staging many art and design exhibitions.

Michele De Lucchi's professional work has always been accompanied by personal research into the themes of the project, design, technology and craftsmanship. In 1990 he created Produzione Privata, a small business within the sphere of which he designs products that, without being commissioned, are created using hand crafting techniques and trade skills.

Among the numerous international awards he has received are the fol-

lowing prizes: Good Design (Japan), Compasso d'Oro, Premio Smau, Office Design Eimu (Italy), Architektur und Office, Deutsche Auswahl, Design Preis Schweiz, Design Zentrum Nordrhein Westfalen, Design Center Stuttgart, Design Plus, Roter Punkt, Design Team of the Year 1997 IF Hannover (Germany), ID Magazine (United States).

In 2000 he was honoured with the title of Officer of the Italian Republic by President Ciampi for merit in the field of design and architecture. In 2001 he was named Full Professor at the Faculty of Design and Arts of the University institute of Architecture in Venice.

Selections of his products are present in the main design museums in Europe, the USA and Japan.

His studio - aMDL Srl - has offices in Milan and Rome.

DESCRIPTION OF THE PROJECTS

pp. 12/13
From notebook no. 29, 1995

Door of Michele De Lucchi's room in the studio at Via Pallavicino, 31 - Milan
Photo: Santi Caleca

p. 14
Architecture of slabs, small notebook no. 1, sketch, pencil on squared paper, 1989

p. 15
TK Project, small notebook no. 10, pencil on paper, Tokyo, 1990

p. 16
Architecture of slabs, crayons on paper, 1989

p. 17
La Fenice, building for offices and shops in Osaka, Japan, 1989-91 - with Tadao Takaichi
Photo: Jun-ichi-Shimomura

Office building for Olivetti in Bari, 1989 - with Nicholas Bewick (in collaboration with Degw)
Photo: Michele De Lucchi

Segments, accessories for the office, Kartell, 1989 - with Tadao Takaichi
Photo: Centro Kappa

p. 18
Sanpo House, Gumma, Japan, 1990 - with Tadao Takaichi
Photo: Michele De Lucchi

p. 19
Sanpo House, small notebook no. 10, sketch, 1990

pp. 20/21
La Fenice, building for offices and shops, view of the staircase, Osaka, Japan, 1989-91 - with Tadao Takaichi
Photo: Jun-ichi-Shimomura

Interior of jails, etching by Giovan Battista Piranesi

Triennale, Documentation Centre, Milan, 1998 - with Brigid Byrne, Filippo Pagliani
Photo: Luca Tamburlini

p. 22
Three houses with square plan, models, 1992
Photo: Federico Brunetti

p. 23
House with square plan, transversal section, crayons and watercolours, 1992

p. 24
Long House, single family residence, watercolours and model, 1990 - with Akiko Takaichi
Photo: Taku Arai

p. 25
Round House, single family residence, watercolours and model, 1990 - with Akiko Takaichi
Photo: Taku Arai

pp. 26/27
Experiments in architecture and Kembo House, 1997-2000
Photo: Alberto Bianchi

p. 28
Restructuring of private residence in Bologna, 1996 - with Alberto Bianchi, Angelo Micheli, Eliana Pasquini
Photo: Michele De Lucchi

p. 29
Villa Sclopis, Hospice and Alzheimer's Centre in Ivrea, 2000 - with Paolo Fromage, Angelo Micheli, Fabiola Minas, Claudio Venerucci

p. 30
Poste Italiane, information kiosks, sketch and photo, 1999 - with Alberto Bianchi, Enrico Quell, Daniele Rossi
Photo: Alberto Novelli

p. 31
Poste Italiane, telebus, sketch, 1999 - with Alberto Bianchi

pp. 32/33
Poste Italiane, Restructuring of the post offices, 1999 - with Bastian Arler, Alberto Bianchi, Angelo Micheli, Enrico Quell, Daniele Rossi, Paola Silva Coronel, Claudio Venerucci
Photo: Santi Caleca

pp. 34/35
Information Centre for Enel electricity plant in Entracque, Cuneo, 1998 - with Sezgin Aksu, Brigid Byrne, Geert Koster, Aya Matsukaze, Filippo Pagliani
Photo: Gabriele Basilico

pp. 36/37
Deutsche Bahn, restructuring of the Reisezentrum, 1995 - with Nicholas Bewick, Brigid Byrne, Michael Corsar, Torsten Fritze, Gladys Escobar, Hanno Giesler, Christian Hartmann, Daniele Rossi, Michele Rossi, Katia Scheika, Steffen Schulz, Alex Strub, Anders Sonnichsen and others
Photo: Joerg Hempel Photodesign

Deutsche Bank, restructuring of the bank branches, 1991 - with Nicholas Bewick
Photo: Gabriele Basilico

Banca 121, financial teleboutique in Lecce, 2001 - with Giovanni Battista Mercurio, Angelo Micheli, Laura Parolin
Photo: Alberto Novelli

Banca Popolare di Lodi, restructuring of the bank branches, 1998 - with Gladys Escobar, Angelo Micheli, Silvia Suardi, Claudio Venerucci
Photo: Santi Caleca

pp. 38/39
Architectural conversion of the Enel electricity plant in Porto Corsini, Ravenna, 2000 - with Carlo De Mattia, Michele Marozzini, Daniele Rossi

Architectural conversion of the Enel electricity plant in La Casella, Piacenza, 2000 - with Brigid Byrne, Gladys Escobar, Federico Seymandi

pp. 40/41
Architectural conversion of the Enel electricity plant, La Spezia, 2001 - with Gladys Escobar, Federico Seymandi

pp. 42/43
Foyer, webcafé at the Teatro Franco Parenti in Milan, 2001 - with Giovanna Latis
Photo: Santi Caleca

pp. 44/45
Architectural conversion of the Enel electricity plant in La Spezia, 2001 - with Gladys Escobar, Federico Seymandi

Architectural conversion of the Enel electricity plant in Porto Corsini, Ravenna, 2000 - with Carlo De Mattia, Michele De Lucchi, Michele Marozzini, Daniele Rossi

pp. 46/47
Office building for Eurogen electricity plant in Chivasso, Turin, 2001 - with Paolo Fromage, Angelo Micheli, Fabiola Minas

p. 48
L'Industria I, crayons and watercolours on cardboard, 2002

p. 49
L'Industria II, crayons and watercolours on cardboard, 2002

p. 50
Macchina minima, pendant lamp, Produzione Privata, 1991 - with Mario Rossi Scola
Photo: Francesco Radino

Tolomeo, table lamp, Artemide, 1986 - with Giancarlo Fassina
Photo: Lorne Liesenfeld

Segno luminoso, competition for Piazzale della Stazione Centrale in Milan, 1999 - with Brigid Byrne, Aya
Photo: Luca Tamburlini

p. 51
Enel high tension pylon, 2000 - Achille Castiglioni, Michele De Lucchi with Sezgin Aksu, Geert Koster
Photo: Luca Tamburlini

Bookcase, Interlubke, 1994 - with Mario Rossi Scola

pp. 52/53
Enel high tension pylon, assembly system, 2000 - Achille Castiglioni, Michele De Lucchi with Sezgin Aksu, Geert Koster

p. 54
Centre of Contemporary Art, competition, Rome, 1999 - Achille Castiglioni, Michele De Lucchi, Italo Lupi with Paolo Bassetti, Fabio Calciati, Filippo Pagliani.
Photo: Luca Tamburlini

p. 55
Competition for the Brescia Fair, 1996 - with Brigid Byrne, Marco Della Torre, Gladys Escobar, Filippo Pagliani
Photo: Luca Tamburlini

Pedestrian Bridge, competition for the Jubilee in Rome, 1998 - with Paolo Bassetti, Brigid Byrne, Fabio Calciati, Filippo Pagliani
Photo: Luca Tamburlini

pp. 56/57
Aria, table lamp for Enel, Produzione Privata, 1997 - with Alberto Nason
Photo: Luca Tamburlini

pp. 58/59
Architectural conversion of the Enel electricity plant in La Casella, Piacenza, 2000 - with Brigid Byrne, Gladys Escobar, Federico Seymandi

Candela, table lamp, Produzione Privata, 1999 - with Alberto Nason
Photo: Luca Tamburlini

p. 60
Liriope, vase from the collection "a che cosa servono i vasi da fiori?", Produzione Privata, 1999 - with Alberto Nason
Photo: Luca Tamburlini

Papavero, vase from the collection "a che cosa servono i vasi da fiori?", Produzione Privata, 1999 - with Alberto Nason
Photo: Luca Tamburlini

p. 61
Hafi, table lamp from the "Sufi" collection, Produzione Privata, 2000 - with Alberto Nason

Nizami, table lamp from the "Sufi" collection, Produzione Privata, 2000 - with Alberto Nason

pp. 62/63
Fatina, table lamp, Produzione Privata, 2001 - with Alberto Nason
Photo: Luca Tamburlini

pp. 64/65
OFX 600, multifunctional fax, Olivetti, 1999 - with Masahiko Kubo
Photo: Luca Tamburlini

Mandarina Duck, shop for clothing and leather goods in Bologna, 1999-2000 - with Angelo Micheli, Silvia Suardi
Photo: Santi Caleca

p. 66
M6, box for computer, Olivetti, 1993 - with Mario Trimarchi
Photo: Tom Vack

p. 67
M6, computer tower, Olivetti, 1993 - with Mario Trimarchi
Photo: Tom Vack

pp. 68/69
Botticelli pittore della Divina Commedia, staging at the Scuderie Papali at the Quirinale in Rome, 2000 - with Enrico Quell, Silvia Suardi
Photo: Alberto Novelli

Office building for Enel electricity plant in Porto Corsini, Ravenna 2001 - with Michele Marozzini, Daniele Rossi

p. 70
M6, box for computer, Olivetti, 1993 - with Mario Trimarchi
Photo: Tom Vack

p. 71
Note book, models, Olivetti, 1994 - with Mario Trimarchi
Photo: Tom Vack

p. 72
Restructuring of private apartment in Milan, 2000 - with Angelo Micheli, Silvia Suardi
Photo: Santi Caleca

Nizami, table lamp from the "Sufi" collection, Produzione Privata, 2000 - with Alberto Nason
Photo: Michele De Lucchi

pp. 74/75
OFX 1000, fax, Olivetti, 1994
Photo: Tom Vack

pp. 76/77
Il Razzo, pencil on paper, 2002

PR2, printer, Olivetti, 1994 - with Johannes Kiessler
Photo: Tom Vack

pp. 78/79
TRI, clothes stand, Poltrona Frau, 2001 - with Philippe Nigro
Photo: Santi Caleca

Palma, exterior lamp, Artemide, 1999 - with Gerhard Reichert
Photo: Elliott Erwitt

Cardboard Tree, staging, 2001 - with Alberto Nason
Photo: Sergio Polano

pp. 80/81
Art Jet 10, printer, Olivetti, 1998 - with Masahiko Kubo

pp. 82/83
Future Vision, research project, Compaq, 1999 - with Sezgin Aksu
Photo: Luca Tamburlini

p. 84
ETP, electronic
typewriter, Olivetti,
1993 - with Alessandro
Chiarato
Photo: Tom Vack

Tolomeo Clamp-On,
lamp, Artemide, 1994
- with Giancarlo Fassina
Photo: Luca Tamburlini

PR2, printer, Olivetti,
1994 - with Johannes
Kiessler
Photo: Tom Vack

p. 85
OFX 300, fax, Olivetti,
2000 - with Masahiko
Kubo

pp. 86/87
Logico, pendant lamp,
Artemide, 2000 - with
Gerhard Reichert
Photo: Elliott Erwitt

pp. 88/89
Enel meter, 2001 - with
Sezgin Aksu
Photo: Mario Carrieri

p. 90
"Bianconi", polystyrene
models created for
products, Olivetti
Photo: Luca Tamburlini

p. 92
At the door of the
Chioso, lithograph,
2000

pp. 94/95
The Chioso, Michele
De Lucchi studio in
Angera, 2000 - with
Angelo Micheli,
Claudio Venerucci
*Photo: Michele
De Lucchi*

p. 96
The Chioso, Michele
De Lucchi studio in
Angera, model, 2000
- with Angelo Micheli,
Claudio Venerucci
Photo: Luca Tamburlini

p. 97
The little house in the
wood, lithograph, 2000

pp. 98/99
Festival Office,
research for an office
building of the future,
1994-95 - with
Alessandro Chiarato,
Mario Trimarchi

pp. 100/101
Puppet, Dog, Face,
experimental
prototypes, Artemide,
1994 - with Mario
Rossi Scola
Photo: Lorne Liesenfeld

p. 102
From small notebook
no. 10, 1990

p. 103
Iris, vase from the
collection "a che cosa
servono i vasi da fiori?",
Produzione Privata,
1999 - with Alberto
Nason
*Photo: Michele
De Lucchi*

pp. 104/105
Invitation card to the
exhibition "A mano
libera: disegni senza
computer", Ivrea, 1999
- with Massimo Canali,
Silvia Suardi

p. 106
Il Trabiccolo,
hypothesis of carriage
to surf the Internet,
1999 - with Stefano
Prina
Photo: Luca Tamburlini

p. 107
Research for a home
cordless telephone,
Siemens, 2000 - with
Sezgin Aksu, Mario
Trimarchi
Photo: Luca Tamburlini

p. 108
Laid Table, La Cerbaia,
Tuscany, 1987
*Photo: Michele
De Lucchi*

p. 109
Reception for NTT
restaurant, Tokyo, 1993
*Photo: Michele
De Lucchi*

p. 110
Artù, system of tables
for the office, Poltrona
Frau, 1999 - with Silvia
Suardi
Advertising campaign
Armando Testa
Photo: Malena Mazza

p. 111
Box for desktop objects,
Poltrona Frau, 1998
Advertising campaign
Armando Testa
Photo: Malena Mazza

pp. 112/113
Piazza di Spagna,
divan, Poltrona Frau,
2000 - with Silvia
Suardi
Photo: Alberto Novelli

pp. 114/115
Kilim Carpets,
watercolours on paper,
2002

pp. 116/117
Christmas Greetings,
cards, 1999, 2000, 2001
- with Massimo Canali

Red Vase, gift for
Christmas 2000
in limited series,
Produzione Privata
- with Alberto Nason
Photo: Luca Tamburlini

Green Vase, gift
for Christmas 2001
in limited series,
Produzione Privata
- with Alberto Nason
Photo: Luca Tamburlini

p. 118
Il Cammino, coloured
pencils on cardboard,
2002

p. 119
From small notebook
no. 10, 1990

p. 120
Portrait of Michele
De Lucchi
Photo: Gitty Darugar